IMAGES
of England

WARBURTON
PARTINGTON AND
CARRINGTON

IMAGES
of England

WARBURTON
PARTINGTON AND
CARRINGTON

Karen Cliff and Vicki Masterson

TEMPUS

Crossroads at Partington, *c.* 1910.

Frontispiece: Aerial photograph of Warburton.

First published 2002
Copyright © Karen Cliff and Vicki Masterson, 2002

Tempus Publishing Limited
The Mill, Brimscombe Port,
Stroud, Gloucestershire, GL5 2QG

ISBN 0 7524 2476 9

Typesetting and origination by
Tempus Publishing Limited
Printed in Great Britain by
Midway Colour Print, Wiltshire

Contents

Bailey Lane, Partington.

Acknowledgements

Pat Southern, Jan Shearsmith, Mr Bob Potts, Mr Tony Wood, *Reed International Publishers*, Mr S.J. Thorne, John Corbridge, Mike Nevell, Robert Nicholls, John Hodgson, Manchester Ship Canal Company, Ben Hargreaves, Simmons Aero films, Derek Chatfield, Mr Boyd, E.J. Morten.

Bibliography

Angus-Butterworth, Lionel, *Old Cheshire Families and Their Seats*, E.J. Morton, 1932.

Bayliss, Don, *Historical Atlas of Trafford*, 1996.

Beamont, William, *Arley Charters*, 1866.

Bolger, Paul, *An Illustrated History of the Cheshire Lines Committee*, Heyday Publishing, 1984.

Breckon, Bill and Jeffrey Parker, *Tracing the History of Houses*.

Cheshire Record Office: miscellaneous land tax records for Cheshire, tithe map of Carrington, miscellaneous deeds and letters relating to Partington and Carrington.

Corbridge, John, *A Pictorial History of the Mersey and Irwell Navigation*, E.J. Morton, 1979.

Dodgson, J.M., *Place Names of Cheshire*.

Engineering (reprinted from) The Manchester Ship Canal, 1894.

Faulkner, Harold, *Warburton 1989*.

Finberg, Joscelyne, *Exploring Villages*, 1998.

Franklyn, J. and J. Tanner, *An Encyclopedic Dictionary of Heraldry*, Pergamon, 1970.

Gray, Ted, *A Hundred Years of the Manchester Ship Canal*, Aurora Publishing, 1994.

Groves, Jill and Pat Higginbottom (transcribers; ed. Jill Groves), *Bowdon Wills Part 2 1651-1689*, 1998.

Harris, Brian, *Cheshire and its Rulers*.

Historical Sketches of Non Conformity in Cheshire.

History of the Cheshire Congregational Union 1806–1906.

Hodgson, J. (ed.), *Estate Papers of the Earls of Stamford*, John Rylands Library, 1995.

Holt, Geoffrey, *A Regional History of the Railways of Great Britain Vol. 10*, David and Charles.

Husain, B.M.C., *Cheshire under the Norman Earls 1066-1237*, Cheshire Community Council, 1973.

Leech, Bosdin, *The History of the Manchester Ship Canal*, Sherratt & Hughes, 1907.

Leycester, Sir Peter, *The History of Cheshire*, 1778.

Manual of the Congregational Church, Bowdon.

Morris, John (ed.), Domesday Book – *Cheshire including Lancashire, Cumbria and north Wales*, 1978.

Nevell, Mike, *Warburton Mill*, University of Manchester Archaeological Unit.

Nevell, Mike, *Archaeology Of Trafford*, University of Manchester Archaeological Unit, 1997.

Newton, T., *Warburton Church and Parish*.

Nicholls, Robert, *Manchester's Narrow Gauge Railways: Chat Moss and Carrington Estates*, Narrow Gauge Railway Society, 1985.

Ordnance Survey, miscellaneous maps of Cheshire.

Ormerod, George, *History of Cheshire*, G. Routledge, 1882.

Parish Record Society, Parish Registers of St Michael's church, Flixton.

Partington Guardian, 1952.

Philip, A.D.M., 'Mossland Reclamation in Nineteenth Century Cheshire', *Historic Society of Lancashire and Cheshire Volume 129, 1980*.

Public Record Office, miscellaneous census records for Carrington and Partington.

Record Society of Lancashire and Cheshire, *Early Cheshire Charters*, 1957.

Renshaw, Charles J., *History of the Church of St. Martin, Ashton on Mersey*.

Renshaw, I.J.E., *Memorials of the Ancient Parish of Ashton on Mersey*.

Richardson, John, *Local Historians Encyclopedia*, Historical Publications Ltd, 1975.

Shell Chemicals, Carrington – Shell.

Stretford and Urmston Journal.

Thorpe, Don, *The Railways of the Manchester Ship Canal*, Oxford Publishing Co., 1984.

Trafford Local Studies Centre, miscellaneous information on Warburton, Carrington and Partington.

Trafford Local Studies Centre, Partington tithe map and apportionment dated 1842.

Trafford Metropolitan Borough Council, *Local History Pack – Altrincham*.

Victoria County, *History of Chester Volume II*.

Visitation of Cheshire, 1533.

Warburton, Norman, *Warburton, the Village and Family*, 1970.

One

Warburton Old Church and Priory

St Werburgh's church at Warburton is a grade one listed building that is one of only twenty-seven timber-framed parish churches in England, eleven of which are in Cheshire and southern Lancashire. It is impossible to say accurately how old the church is. However, there are some clues that may help us to estimate its age.

The Warburton family moved to Arley Hall in1469 and there are several deeds held there that provide invaluable information about the family, church and village. Such a deed shows that in 1170 Roger Fitz Alured granted a moiety of 'Werbertune' to Adam de Dutton upon his marriage to his daughter Agnes. In 1190 Adam gave this moiety, with his wife's consent, to the Norbertine White Canons of Premontre, Normandy, who founded a priory there by a deed reading, 'I, Adam de Dutton have consented with my wife Agnes to give to God, St Mary and St Werburgh and to the Canons of the Premonstratensian Order here serving God, a moiety of the vill of Warburton in free alms…'

It seems likely that there was a church there before the Norbertines arrived, as there is an 1194 deed in which a William Boydele refers to a gift he previously made to 'God and St Werburgh and her Chapel at Werberton' whilst he was priest there. However, we cannot be sure that the church was, as is mooted, of Saxon origins. Dr Mike Nevell in his 1999 survey of Warburton church states that the double dedication of the church in 1187-90 to St Mary and St Werburgh may indicate a Norman pre-dedication to the Saxon saint St Werburgh. The shape of the graveyard, which is curved with a surrounding bank, similar to some that have been found in pre-Conquest sites in Wales, also suggests that this church may be of Anglo-Saxon origin.

The monks did not stay long at Warburton. It is not known why they returned to their motherhouse in Cockersand. In an undated deed, Abbott Roger gave back the gift of the moiety to Geoffrey de Dutton, son of Adam, and in 1271 the Abbot of Cockersand transferred to Geoffrey the chapel and the right to appoint a cleric, freeing the church from the bounds of the Norburtines. There is no trace of the priory buildings, but the field next to the rectory is called Abbey Field.

Warburton has historically been connected to the parish of Lymm and up to the seventeenth century the priest at Warburton divided his time between the two, serving Warburton each Sunday and Lymm every other Sunday. However, in 1868 Warburton was separated from Lymm parish and from then on stood on its own. In 1538 Thomas Cromwell introduced a Mandate saying that every parish should purchase a 'sure coffer', or secure chest. A book, in which the parson was to enter every christening, burial and marriage that he had undertaken, was to be placed in this chest and kept locked, with only the church warden and the parson holding the keys. The entries were to be made after the service on Sunday, with the church warden as witness. Thus were the beginnings of the parish chest. The earliest registers to survive at Warburton are seventeenth century and the first entry was a christening in 1611. There are about 1,500 parishes whose registers begin in 1538. Most entries were made on paper at first and not put into a book until the 1590s, so the entry at Warburton is quite an early one.

Warburton church was originally constructed with a strong timber frame with wattle and daub, probably on the site of the present nave. The church has had several stages in its development, the first being in the twelfth century when the first trusses were erected. The second set of trusses was probably erected in the early thirteenth century when the church was enlarged. This could have been around the time of the sale of the priory site back to the manorial lord. Manchester University Archaeological Unit have dated these huge oak trusses that support the roof to the late thirteenth or early fourteenth century. The oldest wall would appear to be the north wall. 1645 is the first recorded restoration. The south and west walls were rebuilt in Runcorn sandstone and the roof covered with flags replacing the thatch. The oak pillars were covered in plaster and painted.

In 1722 the church was flagged and 'beautified' and a gallery made, according to the account of Arnold Drinkwater, the family bailiff. In 1813 alterations and repairs were made with timber bought from Liverpool, which cost £64 and was used to re-floor the church. Before this the floor was covered with rushes which were refreshed once a year on the first Monday of August, which was called Rushbearing Monday. There was a fair and horse races on this day. The church was also fitted out with new pews. A new vestry was built and the old vestry opened into the church, making an extension to the little chancel. The southern side of the church was rebuilt in brick. In 1830 the whole of the inside of the church was whitewashed. Two women were paid £1 3s 5d for sixteen and a half days work in the church after this had been done. In 1857 Revd Beaufort tried to modernize the church by flooring the sacrarium and chancel with tiles that covered up some of graves of previous rectors.

In 1894 dry rot was discovered and an appeal was launched. The pews that had been installed in 1813 were taken out. In 1897 the roof was repaired by Henry Thomas of Oughtrington.

In 1880 plans were made to rebuild the old church but such were the objections that it was decided that a new church would be built in Bent Lane. The Cheshire record office holds plans, letters and other documents relating to the building of the church. most of which are from John Douglas and the Warburtons of Arley. Mr Douglas was the architect who designed the new church. He was considered an important architect of his time and also designed the church house, the schoolhouse and the post office. His use of traditional building materials ensures that these buildings are in keeping with the other buildings in the village. The church furniture and hassocks were supplied by West and Collier of Hambledon. The church was dedicated in 1885 by William Stubbs, Bishop of Chester, and the old church ceased to be the parish church.

In 1927 deathwatch beetles were found to have caused disastrous damage to the old church, but with the help of the Ancient Monuments Society, the church was restored. The Manchester City News opened a subscription that enabled the purchase of the old oak beams from Birch Hall, Rusholme, which was being demolished. This new timber replaced the old rotted beams. The roof was also repaired, at a cost of £750. It was agreed that a brass tablet should be placed in on the south wall of the nave to record the restoration of the church in memory of Revd G. Egerton Warburton, rector 1872-1919. There is also an alabaster tablet on the north wall of the new church in memory of the same.

Unfortunately, in 1958 the deathwatch beetle returned, and an appeal for £2000 was launched. Once again the church was saved at a cost of £1300, the rest of the money being used to construct a car park and do renovation work on the graveyard. During the replacement of the floorboards with stone flags in the little chancel, several bones were found. They were sent to Manchester University for analysis and were found to be the bones of a male buried around 1700. They were buried again before the new floor was laid.

St Werburgh's old church as it stands today. The church was probably originally rectangular. The steeple, vestry and part of the chancel were built in 1711. The bell that hangs in the tower weighs around six hundredweight and is held in a frame and wheel of solid oak. It was cast in 1575 so either the bell was bought second hand or the tower was preceded by an older one in which the bell hung.

The north wall of St Werburgh's old church, Warburton. These walls, together with the pillars, are the oldest part of the church, probably because it is protected from the worst of the weather. The bricked-up door is medieval. The interior of this wall had text painted or stencilled on it.

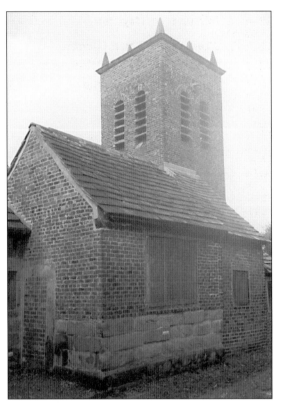

According to Arnold Drinkwater's diaries, the church was flagged and a gallery was fitted in 1722. Arnold, the Warburton family bailiff, helped make the gallery himself, and the bricked-up door which led to the gallery stairs can be seen in this photograph. The gallery was removed in 1857. The floor of the little chancel was repaired in 1958 as the wooden flooring had succumbed to dry rot. Several bones were found which proved to be those of a man buried around 1700. The bones were re-interred before the new flagstones were laid.

The bricked-up door on the north side of the church from inside. This door was filled in around the time that the gallery was built. While the door that was restored has a semi-circular top, older sketches show it to have a pointed arch The window above the door is assumed to be pre-1645.

The list of rectors of Warburton old church as given by T. Newton.

In 1895 the pews that had been put in the church in 1813, as part of a renovation of the woodwork in the church, were found to be suffering from woodworm and were taken out. The best of the pews were salvaged and put in the north side of the church and the little chancel. This photograph taken by H. Wilkinson shows the interior of the church before the pews were removed, and the great oak trusses that supported the original building can also be clearly seen. The window in the chancel was installed in 1857 at a cost of £29 and was designed by Wailes of Newcastle. It is unusual in that the centre panel represents the Resurrection and not the Crucifixion as is the norm.

11—	...	William de Boydele.
1100	to	
1271	...	Norbertine White Canons.
1278	...	Robertus de Dentone.
1292	...	John de Budworth.
1328	...	William de Warburton.
1367	...	Petrus de Shawe.
1391	...	John Byrkin.
1432	...	Roger Domville.
1454	...	Jacobus Gladelyf.
1458	...	Richard Chonal.
1486	...	Roger Chapman.
1509	...	John Fernehead.
1524	...	Richard Warburton.
15—	...	Thomas Warburton.
1597	...	Edward Shelmerdine.
1627	...	William Bispham.
16—	...	Richard Grimshey.
1669	...	Joseph Bradley.
1698	...	James Thompson, A.B.
1714	...	John Yates.
1732	...	Timothy Featherstonehaugh.
1766	...	Robert Massie, A.M.
1778	...	George Heron, A.M.
1832	...	J. F. Egerton-Warburton, A.M.
1850	...	D. A. Beaufort, M.A.
1872	...	Geoffrey Egerton-Warburton, M.A.
1919	...	C. D. Lewis, M.A.
1930	...	A. Hoyle, L.Th.
1934	...	S. J. Lloyd Jones, B.A.

St Werburgh's churchyard. There is some evidence that the graveyard is medieval, such as its curved shape and the bank surrounding it. The retaining wall on the south east side was completed in 1845. Before this the churchyard sloped down to the green. The boundary fence was at one time divided into 4ft lengths and each length allocated to a villager who would be responsible for its upkeep. In Arnold Drinkwater's diary there is a rough map of the churchyard showing these lengths. There were originally four entrances to the graveyard, the remaining two being the main entrance and the gate through to the rectory garden on the west side of the church. The other entrances were stiles situated in the north and south corners of the churchyard. The oldest visible gravestone is that of Margaret Leigh who was buried in 1683. The earliest entry in the surviving registers of burials dates from 1638. However, there were probably many earlier burials. In 1865, three stone coffins were found to the north of the church, which were said by some to date back to the Norbertine monks. There are also many graves inside the church, including those of five rectors and four members of the Drinkwater family. The graveyard was extended in 1903 to include some of the rectory garden, and in 1932 the retaining wall on the south-east side was built and the chestnut and other trees were planted.

The tower is at the east end of the church and bears the date 1711. It was built with money given by the parishioners in the form of a special mize or rate. It is made of brick, is 35ft high and has windows on each side. At the bottom of the tower is an oak door, which has a spy hole in it through which the graveyard could be watched, and any body snatchers detected. The tower houses a bell, which has the date 1575 on it – presumably the date it was cast. The bell weighs six hundredweight and is $2\frac{1}{2}$ft in diameter. It is decorated with fleur-de-lys and has the initials R.B. engraved on it. A sturdy oak ladder, the timber of which was purchased from the Earl of Stamford in 1804, was put into the steeple. However the bell frame is now unsafe and the bell can no longer be rung.

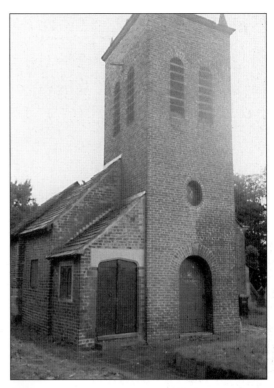

The sundial, which was purchased in 1769. The church accounts state that the cost of the pedestal and the placing of it was £1 15s 10d. The dial itself bears the date 1765 and there is no mention of the cost. Beyond the dial can be seen the gate to the one time rectory, which has been renovated. It is said that the inhabitants of this rectory found the remains of a stone floor and some charred beams 8ft down in the garden which was thought to be part of the Norbertine priory. A ghost of a Norbertine monk is said to haunt the old rectory.

The date stone on the south side of the church reading 1645, which was the time when the church was much extended. The southern and western walls of the nave were rebuilt in stone and the roof of the nave probably lowered and covered in stone slate. The little chancel and the vestry were added to the southern side of the nave. William Warburton of Warburton Park probably built the aisle on the north side of the church, as it is called Park Pews.

The hexagonal pulpit is made of oak decorated with conventional Elizabethan designs. It is thought to date from around 1600. The carving is said to be either Jacobean or Elizabethan and is similar to the panelling in Bent Farm on Bent Lane which was built in around 1600. The pulpit was originally situated by the cluster of trusses in the south-east end of the church but was moved in 1857. It now stands on the north-east side of the church. This photograph shows the interior of the north and east walls of the church with the huge oak beams in the foreground and the area known as park pews. The old stone coffins that were found in the graveyard were once located here.

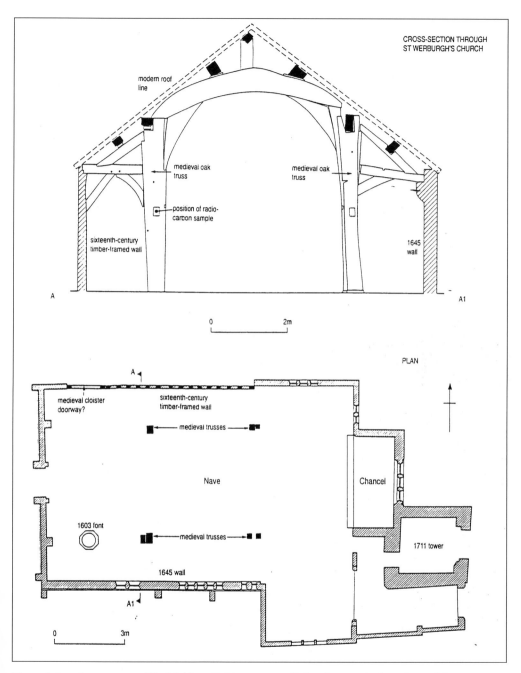

CROSS-SECTION THROUGH
ST WERBURGH'S CHURCH

modern roof line

medieval oak truss

medieval oak truss

position of radio-carbon sample

sixteenth-century timber-framed wall

1645 wall

A

A1

0   2m

PLAN

medieval cloister doorway?

sixteenth-century timber-framed wall

medieval trusses

A

Nave

Chancel

1603 font

medieval trusses

1645 wall

A1

1711 tower

0   3m

Plan of church courtesy of Dr M. Nevell, University of Manchester Archaeological Department. Here we see a cross section of the church showing the nave, the chancel, the little chancel and the tower.

This is one of the three stone coffins said to have been found in the churchyard. George Ormerod records in his *History of Cheshire* (under the date August 9 1816) that three coffin-shaped gravestones were discovered, describing them as 7ft, 8ft and 3ft long respectively. The soil was removed and they were found to be the lids of three coffins. One of these coffins was opened to reveal a tall skeleton, which turned to dust as soon as the coffin was opened. There is no evidence to verify the skeleton and as the cover of the coffin was in bad shape and not airtight it seems unlikely that any contents would survive. The interior of the coffin is shaped to that of a man. There is another account which says that in 1865 the then sexton was probing the ground on the north side of the church when he hit something solid, and the coffin was brought out of the ground then. Whatever the true story, the coffin is thought to be of medieval origin and could have contained the remains of an inhabitant of the priory. Some say that the 3ft coffin could be that of John de Dutton, son of Adam de Dutton, who was buried at Warburton in the twelfth century. The Ordnance Survey map of Cheshire (number XVII 3, 1873), shows the spot where the three coffins were found. This coffin was leant against the side of the church but was brought inside in 1887 as it was being damaged by vandals.

The Lych gate was put in place in memory of Alderman James Craven of Manchester by his son in 1888. It replaces a gate and stone stumps which were moved to the west entrance of the graveyard near the rectory.

The font, which is made out of sandstone, used to be on the north side of the church but in 1898 it was moved to the south side, from where the pews had been removed due to woodworm. It had been painted but on removal of the paint the date 1603 was found. The base of the font does not match the hexagonal shape of the top. In its original position it was surrounded by pews so the shape would have better fitted into the space. The wooden lid to the font is in Warburton new church. The inscription on the font says 'Richard Drinkwater, the Keeper'. There is a faint date of 1602 on the other side. However, the oak cover that fits exactly is dated 1595, so the font was more likely inscribed at the later date.

The yew tree is in the far north-east of the churchyard. It is said to be over 1000 years old and to have been used to make some of the bows of the Cheshire archers who fought at Agincourt and the Wars of the Roses. It has certainly been pollarded at some point to encourage new growth, which would have been ideal for bows. It measured 18ft round in its prime.

The church door. This is now the main entrance to the church, located on the west side of the building. The door was made in 1645, although the door on the north side was maintained until 1722 when the gallery was built.

Warburton church boundary dig, 1998.

Door to the tower. Here we can see the door to the tower and to the vestry. In the forefront is a cluster of trusses, which show how the church was extended.

Archers Field. Opposite the church, Archers Field is said to be the field that the archers practiced in.

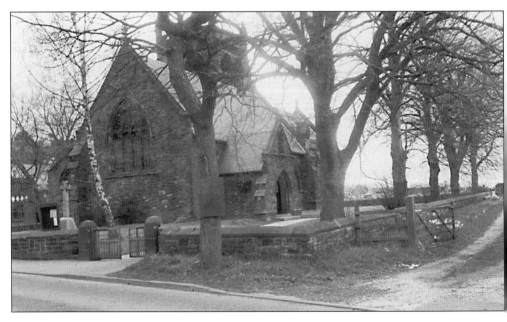

The new church. In 1880 the old church was going to be rebuilt but the then rector, Mr R.E. Egerton Warburton, was against the proposed new plans as it would have completely changed the shape of the church. The new church cost £9,000 and was funded totally by Mr R.E. Egerton Warburton.

The new church, which seats 300, is built in the perpendicular style in Runcorn sandstone, like the chapel at Arley Hall. It consists of the chancel, nave, north aisle, south-west porch and north-east embattled tower containing eight bells. There is a stained-glass window on the east wall, permission for which was given in January 1888 and represents the Passion of Our Lord. On the north wall of the chancel is an alabaster tablet in memory of Revd G. Egerton Warburton, which was made by Robert Bridgeman & Sons of Lichfield.

The church hall was erected in 1889. It was designed by John Douglas, who was also the architect for the church, the schoolhouse and the post office in Warburton.

Interior of the new church, showing the parish chest, the nave and the stained-glass window.

The parish chest in the new church. This chest is made of slabs of oak 1½ inches thick. There are three locks and three keys held by the priest, the church warden and the treasurer. Inside it is divided into two, with two separate lids. Originally the parish registers and other important parish documents were kept inside, but most of these have now been deposited at the Cheshire record office. In his diary, Arnold Drinkwater, the town bailiff, writes '1719, the church chest made about this time, £1 6s 6d'. However, it would seem to be much older. It was originally in the old church but now resides in the new one.

The font in the new church. This font cover exactly fits the font in the old church. It is octagonal rising to a point with a square top and pinnacles. The date 1595 is carved on one face and letters inscribed on the other side for which there is no evidential explanation, unless they are the initials of the then church officials.

Constable's handcuffs, which are kept in the parish chest.

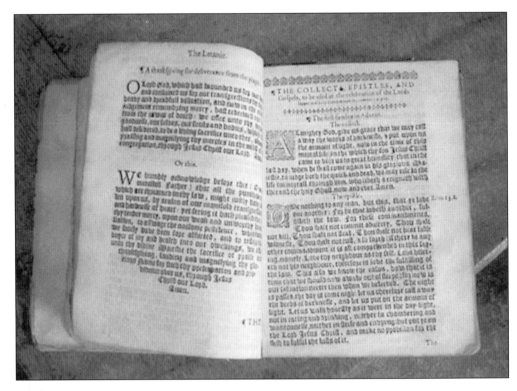

Book of service that is kept in the parish chest.

Two

Gentry and Landowners

The Warburton family is an ancient family, which can be traced back many centuries. The family members were at times extremely prominent in the history of Cheshire, if not in that of the nation. Some were brave knights who battled for king and country, and many were great landowners and entrepreneurs, and although their residence at Warburton was relatively brief, the name lives on in the area as a strong reminder of the past.

Before the Norman Conquest, when William the Conqueror came over to Britain from Normandy to take the throne from King Harold, Warburton was divided into two halves or moieties. One moiety was held by Ernwy and the other by Raven, who were both Saxon freemen. At the time of the conquest, King William divided the country between his followers. Cheshire was put into the care of Hugh of Avranches or Hugh Lupus, the cousin of King William and a very powerful man. Cheshire was a frontier county, as most of Lancashire and certainly Wales had not been subdued by the Normans. It was therefore important to have a strong leader. One such man was William Fitz Nigel, Baron of Halton and one of Hugh's most trusted followers. He was was given Ernwy's moiety in order to ensure its safety against attack from Lancashire. Osborne, son of Tezzo, another of Hugh's men and said to be the ancestor of the Boydells of Dodleston (Ormerod, *History of Cheshire*), was given Raven's moiety. It was the practice to have a seneschal or steward to look after the land and William Fitz Nigel gave this position to Odard de Dutton, who came over with the conquest and was a direct ancestor of Adam de Dutton. The Warburton family descended from Odard via Adam. Nigel gave Odard a sword of office, as was the custom in those days, which became a family heirloom. Unfortunately, although the sword survived many generations, no one knows where it is now.

Adam de Dutton, great-grandson of Odard, was a good businessman and became an important and powerful man. His name is to be seen on many of the deeds and charters of the time. He was made seneschal of Widnes and Blackburnshire and as such had great judicial powers. By the time of Richard I, he had come into possession of both halves of Warburton. One half, being of the fee of Halton, was given to Adam de Dutton by John, Constable of Chester. The other half was of the fee of Boydell and, according to Ormerod's *History of Cheshire*, was conferred on Adam de Dutton on the occasion of his marriage to Agnes, by her father, Robert Fitz Alured, with the permission of his son and heir, William. It is this portion that Adam later gave to the White Cannons of St Norbert (charter 68 – see page 32).

Adam's son Geoffrey fought in the Third Crusade with his superior John Lacy, constable of Chester and eighth Baron of Halton. He was obviously successful, as he was knighted and granted the symbol of a Saracen's head as part of the Warburton crest. He had a son, also Geoffrey, during whose lifetime the land given by Adam de Dutton to the Norbertine monks was returned, and he settled in Warburton in 1248. This Geoffrey is referred to in several documents as Lord de Warburton and it is suggested that he built and resided in Warburton Park.

Sir Peter de Dutton, the grandson of Geoffrey, was one of the first Duttons to assume the de Warburton name. It was quoted in the *London and Middlesex Illustrated* in 1749: 'Sir Peter de Dutton knt., being possessed of the town and Lordship of Warburton...he made it his chief house and thence wrote himself de Warburton which name hath ever since been retained by his successors'. This Warburton knew the importance of fisheries and raised a weir at Warburton on the river Mersey. He died before 1314 and was succeeded by Geoffrey de Warburton who was made Sheriff of Lancashire in 1326.

Warburton Park remained the principal seat of the Warburton family until 1469, when Sir Peter Warburton built the house at Arley to which the family removed, although a branch of the family remained at Warburton until the late 1600s. The Warburtons of Arley continued in succession until the death of Sir Peter Warburton in 1813, when the estate was left in trust to Rowland Eyles Egerton Warburton, who was at that time a minor. The Warburton family were still the main landowners, as can be seen in the Tithe apportionment of 1837.

The ancient house of Carrington is one of the few families that can prove their descent from the time of the Norman Conques,t and a branch of the original family still continues to this day. The pedigree, which is registered at the Royal College of Arms, confirms the family descent for over 800 years.

The original founder of the Carrington house in England was a Hamo de Carenton, the younger son of the Marquis de Carenton of Normandy in France. Hamo de Carenton came over to Britain around the time of the Norman Conquest in 1066. The de Carenton family possessed large estates in Normandy, and the name Carenton/Carrington is believed to have been taken from the town and port of Carenton in that region. Hamo de Carenton was also a nephew of Hamo de Massey and as a young man he fought alongside his uncle at the Battle of Hastings in 1066. Hamo de Massey was rewarded for his services to the new King, William the Conqueror, with lands in Dunham, Ashley, Bowdon, Hale, Baguley and Ollerton. Hamo de Massey went on to grant his nephew, Hamo de Carenton, with the gift of a manor in the parish of Bowdon, which may have been as a reward for his personal services and assistance during the battle.

The manor was situated in Bowdon, Cheshire, about eight miles south of Manchester, and was bordered along one side by the river Mersey. It included a large area of land suitable for farming, woodland and around 500 acres of moss land. Hamo de Carenton decided to settle in the area and went on to build himself and his family a manor house. The manor house became known as Carrington Hall and the village, which eventually developed around it, took on the name of Carrington.

The manor and village of Carrington were not included in the Domesday survey of 1086, so probably developed some time after this date, although there may have been some settlement in the area from an earlier period, which was not recorded. There are many differing theories on the origin of the name Carrington, such as Karen's tun (Karen's farm), named after a Dane, Karen who may have settled in the area around the eighth century. However, the known facts are that the Carrington family did settle in the area around the eleventh century, and details of its history originate from this time.

The fame and fortune of the Carrington family can be traced through many of the documents and charters which have survived throughout the years. In the twelfth century Sir Jordan de Carenton, who at the time was serving as a knight to Ranulph de Gernon the fourth Earl of Chester, took part in the Battle of Lincoln, where on 2 February 1141, King Stephen was captured.

Carrington Family

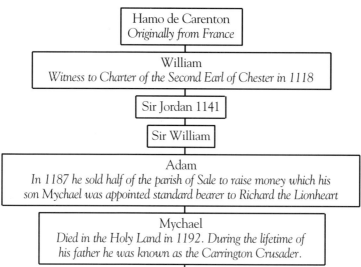

| Hamo de Carenton |
| *Originally from France* |

| William |
| *Witness to Charter of the Second Earl of Chester in 1118* |

| Sir Jordan 1141 |

| Sir William |

| Adam |
| *In 1187 he sold half of the parish of Sale to raise money which his son Mychael was appointed standard bearer to Richard the Lionheart* |

| Mychael |
| *Died in the Holy Land in 1192. During the lifetime of his father he was known as the Carrington Crusader.* |

| William 1240 |
| *Son of Mychael who had died in the Holy Land. Lord of the Manor of Carrington and Ashton juxta Carrington. He married Cicely the daughter of Hamo de Massey.* |

The Carrington family were loyal supporters of the crown and during the twelfth century were involved in the religious wars that became known as the Crusades. Adam de Carrington left his manor in England to make the difficult and often perilous journey to the Holy Land to fight, while his son Mychael followed him at a later date. The King, Richard Coeur de Lion was so impressed by Mychael that he appointed him as a royal standard-bearer. This position incurred considerable expense for his father, Adam, who in order to raise the necessary money to provide his son with the required accoutrements, sold half of the manor of Sale to Adam de Dutton, the Seneschal of Blackburn. The original deed for the sale survives and is now part of the Arley Hall collection of charters. Unfortunately Mychael was killed while fighting in the Holy Land, but an effigy of him still remains, and can be seen in the church of St John the Baptist in Chester. Mychael is depicted as a knight in chain mail, and the effigy was named after him as the Carrington Crusader. On the death of Adam de Carrington, the estate passed to his grandson William, who was the son of Mychael. In 1240 William was described as 'Lord of the Manor of Carington and Ashton juxta Carington'.

The Carrington family also owned over two thirds of Ashton on Mersey and in 1304 a John de Carrington who was the lord of the manor, along with William de Sala, built the church of St Martin's in Ashton on Mersey.

The manor of Carrington was considerable both in size and importance; this was reflected in 1432, when Sir William Carrington travelled across to France in order to fight for his country. His retinue consisted of ten men-at-arms and included fifty archers. The fact that he was able to take with him such a large band of retainers emphasised the importance and wealth of the Carrington estate.

In 1553 the lord of the manor Sir John Carrington died, leaving an estate that included Carrington Hall, one water mill, 200 acres of cultivated land, forty acres of meadow, sixty acres of pasture, three acres of wood and 500 acres of moor, moss and turf. The total acreage amounted to over 800. He also left a gold chain and in his will stated that this heirloom should only pass through the male line of the family. His son John, who inherited the estate aged thirteen, went on to marry Ellen, the daughter of Thomas Holford of Holford and they produced one daughter, Jane, who was born in around 1562.

In 1577 Sir John Carrington died leaving no male heir. His daughter Jane, by then aged fifteen, had been married to George Booth of Dunham Massey only a month before her father's death, possibly as a way of securing the Carrington estate in the event of there being no male heir. Jane however died childless in 1591 and soon after her death her husband claimed the Carrington estate on behalf of the Booth family of Dunham. With the death of Jane, the Carrington family finally lost the rights to the Carrington estate where they had been lords of the manor for over four hundred years. Despite a legal suit from the remaining members of the Carrington family the estate remained in the hands of the Booth family and was eventually to become part of the Stamford estate.

Some of the remaining members of the Carrington family continued to live in the surrounding area and a small number of them settled in the Flixton area, on the Lancashire side of the river Mersey. They settled in the Shaw Town area of Flixton and farmed the land there. The estates they owned gradually became divided and sold off as members of the family died. The last remaining landowner in the Flixton area was William Carrington, who died in 1814.

The Carrington family worshipped in the chapel situated in Carrington Hall or at the church of St Mary's in Bowdon, where they had a private chapel. Some of the family used St Martin's in Ashton on Mersey, or St Michael's in Flixton, where the parish registers include many references to the name of Carrington. It was reputed that a Lady Carrington was responsible for building the first bridge over the river Mersey into Flixton, so the villagers of Carrington could attend St Michael's church without getting their feet wet crossing the Mersey.

The manor of Carrington included fertile land suitable for farming, and a large area of moss land. During the eleventh century Hamo de Carrington decided to live on the manor and oversee the running of his estate, and was probably responsible for the building of the manor house, which became known as Carrington Hall. Carrington Hall was sited close to the river Mersey and was built some time around the end of the eleventh century but there are no definite recorded dates available so we can only speculate. It was not included in the Domesday Book so it may have been built some time after 1086. It was to become the family home of the Carringtons for over four hundred years. The location of the hall, so close to the river Mersey, ensured that there would always be an adequate supply of fresh water necessary both for farming and the general day-to-day running of the manor, while at the same time it provided food and an additional form of transport to the road, which was probably at times unusable. The river Mersey also provided a natural boundary between Cheshire and Lancashire, which meant that Carrington could be defended with ease from any trouble arising in the north.

The building, and later the day-to-day running of a manor house would have attracted many people to the area in search of work. These people would have either lived in the hall itself or close by. As more houses were built to accommodate them, the village of Carrington would have gradually begun to take shape.

Carrington Hall would have been like many other English manor houses of the period. It was most probably a rectangular building with two floors; the upper floor or solar would have been where all the business of the manor was dealt with, while the family would have lived on the lower floor, which would also have been used for storage. An external staircase would have linked the two floors. Over the years the hall would have had many additions and improvements and there is evidence to suggest that it had a private chapel for the Carrington family. In 1378 Sir William de Carington obtained a private license from the Bishop of Litchfield in order for religious services to be held within the hall.

When Lady Jane Carrington died in 1591 and the Carrington estate passed over to the Booth family of Dunham Massey, The new Lord of the Manor, George Booth, decided to lease Carrington Hall and the Carrington estate. The hall then passed through various tenants, one of the earliest being Robert Tipping, who until his death in 1622 was described as one of the richest men in the area. His inventory taken in 1623 shows he was responsible for the addition of a bedchamber and a dining chamber to the hall. The hall was described as 'as an Elizabethan structure comprising a portion considerably older' (Ormerod).

The land tax returns for the late eighteenth century list Joshua Cragg 1780-1803 and Alan Cragg 1806-1828 as tenants, with the owner as the Earl of Stamford. In the year 1818 the Stamford estate papers list an account for repairs, which were carried out on Carrington Hall, Carrington Mill and demesne, including repairs to the banks and floodgates of the river Mersey. The cost was £54 17s 11d. From 1829 the land tax returns list William Walkden and his family as occupiers of the hall, while the owner is listed as Lord Stamford.

The Tithe map for Carrington, dated 1842, describes the hall as 'Carrington Hall and Pleasure Grounds'. It was surrounded by an orchard and a kitchen garden and included a farmyard and outbuildings. Although the Walkden family continued to farm the Carrington estate until around 1900, Carrington Hall gradually fell into disrepair and was eventually demolished some time around 1846-59, although the exact date is not clear and all references give slightly different dates. The *History and Gazetteer of Cheshire*, 1860, says the Hall was 'Taken down 1849', while Kelly's Directory of Cheshire, 1864, says 'The ancient hall was taken down about 1856, and replaced by a handsome farm residence'.

There does appear to be some confusion over where Carrington Hall was originally situated. Around the time it was demolished, 1846-59, the Walkden family, who were the tenants during this period, may have transferred from Carrington Hall to the farm buildings, which were known confusingly as Carrington Hall Farm. The Walkden family continued to be listed on the census under Carrington Hall/farm. The farm buildings were situated close to the main road, which runs through the centre of the village whereas the hall itself was situated much closer to the river Mersey. It is possible that over the intervening years the location of Carrington Hall may have become confused with that of Carrington Hall Farm, as they were located relatively close to each other. Comparison with the Tithe map of 1838 and the Ordnance Survey map of 1896 (sheet number CX.6), shows clearly that the location of Carrington Hall and Carrington Hall Farm was quite separate. From 1923 Carrington Hall Farm was occupied and farmed by Tom Bradbury-Mayer, until Petrocarbon Ltd took over the area for development in 1940.

Partington Hall was situated close to the river Mersey in the village of Partington, and was originally part of the Dunham Massey estate. There is very little information available relating to the hall and its history but we do know that it was leased out to various tenants throughout its life. It was used as a farmhouse, with the tenants farming the adjoining land included in the Partington estate. The hall may have been built sometime during the seventeenth century or possibly much earlier. We do know that it was in existence in 1780 as the land tax returns for that year list the proprietor of the hall as a Mr John Barratt, with the occupier as a Mr George Williamson.

The land tax was a levy placed on land that had an annual value of more than twenty shillings and was initially collected from 1693. Early land tax records have not survived, but from 1780, when duplicate copies were produced, they have, and provide a useful aid to research.

Although the information given by the land tax records provides us with some information about the estate, it does not present a clear picture as to who actually owned the hall. The estate was probably sub-let, and it must be noted, moreover, that the proprietor was not always the freeholder of the land, but could instead have been a copyholder or even a long leaseholder, while the occupier of property may have been a tenant or even a sub-tenant. Using the land tax records as a point of reference, it is clear that from 1780 to 1785 a Mr George Williamson occupied the Hall, the proprietor being Mr John Barratt. The occupancy was then transferred to the Worthington family and from 1797 until 1803 the occupier was listed as a Betty Worthington with the proprietor as Mr Clubb. After that date, the occupancy transferred over to John Worthington, who was probably a son or other close relative of Betty Worthington. John Worthington occupied the Hall and farmed the estate until his death around 1841-42. He is listed on the Tithe map apportionment for Partington, which is dated 1841, as the occupier, with the landowner listed as Mr John Barratt.

The hall is described on the Tithe apportionment as a house and garden. In his will dated 16 December 1841 John Worthington wrote: 'I give and bequeath unto my dear wife Margaret the use and enjoyment of such of my household goods plate china linen and furniture as she shall make choice of during her life and I also give and bequeath to my said wife and her assigns the yearly sum of thirty pounds to be paid to her and her assigns by equal half yearly payments.' It continues, 'I give and bequeath the several legacies following to wit my daughter Martha Worthington my sons The

William Worthington and Joseph Worthington each the sum of one hundred pounds and to my grandchildren Hugh Worthington John Erlam and Mary Erlam the children of my late daughter Elizabeth Erlam the like sum of one hundred pounds to be divided between them in equal shares'. He goes on to say that 'all my farming stock and implements and utensils in husbandry and that my said children Martha Worthington William Worthington and Joseph Worthington shall have the option of taking the same at such valuation to be paid by them to my said executors at the expiration of six calendar months from my decease but in case they decline or refuse to take the same of such valuation then I direct the same household goods furniture farming stock and other personal effects to be sold by my executors'.

The estate papers for the Stamford estate make a reference to the fifth Earl of Stamford placing the Partington Hall estate up for auction in the year 1813. To do this he employed a surveyor, Mr Edward Stelfox to estimate the value of the estate, which included the hall and adjoining farmland. In total the estate amounted to 56 acres 0 rods and 10 perches. The hall, orchard and gardens were valued at £5 per annum while the whole estate was valued at £3430 17s 6d with a total yearly value of £122 10s 7d. Only a portion of the estate was sold at auction; the land agent for the Earl of Stamford, Mr Hugo Worthington, who was a witness to the sale, reported that 'only four lots out of the total estate were sold with most of the estate remaining unsold'. The unsold lots, which possibly included Partington Hall, were subsequently withdrawn.

The actual ownership of the hall, however, is still not clear, as different proprietors are listed at different dates, but it is probably safe to assume that the hall was always part of the Stamford estate and was leased out. Most of the field names, which were listed as lots in the sale of 1813, corroborate this as they appeared in the auction of 1813 as lifelong leases. There is no further reference to Partington Hall in the estate papers and the hall may have been sold by private treaty at a later date.

Partington Hall was to remain in the occupancy of the Worthington family who continued to farm the land until the 1920s. The hall was eventually demolished and today all that remains is the road name Hall Lane to remind us of a time long gone.

BOX.	NO.	DATE.	PARTIES.	SUBJECT.	PLACE.	WITNESSES.
1	68	Abt. 1170.	Roger fitz Alured, with the confent of Wm. his fon and heir, to Adam de Dutton & Agnes, Roger's daur.	Grant of half Werbertune in frank marriage, doing for it the foreign fervice of 1-10th of a knight's fee, to the grantor's chief lord.	Warburton.	Henry, prior of Norton, John, conftable of Chefter, Hugh de Dutton, Rich. Fitun, John fitz Alured, Wm. de Carintun, Rob. Leon, Robert Venator, Wrenou Punterlin, Geoff. de Merigg, Geoff. de Duttun, Geoff. de Staalee, Aufred fitz Lanſ, Wm. de Boun, brother David.
1	6	Abt. 1173.	John, conftable of Chefter, to Adam de Dutton.	Confirmation of the above grant No. 68.	Warburton.	H., prior of Norton, Roger fitz Alured, Rich. Fitun, Hugh de Dutton, Robert Venator, Friar David.
1	95a	The fame.	The fame.	Grant of Richard de Stretton (a bondman) and all his children.	Stretton.	Hugh de Dutton, John fitz Alured, Wrenna, Radulf, Hanſelin, Wm. de Canult, R. Burdon, Alured fitz Jan., Rich. Starki, Wm. de Buhu, Gregory Luffuc, Rich. Maltalent, Ranechol le Runus, Galfrid, the clerk who wrote the charter.
4	1	1187.	Garnerius de Neapolis, prior of St. John of Jerufalem, in England, with the confent of his chapter, to Adam de Dutton.	Grant of the mediety of Warburton, wh. the prior and chapter had by the gift of John, conftable of Chefter, for his and the fouls of their anceftors, and grant of 2 bovates in Wiveton, and 12 lands there, and 1 falt-houfe in Northwich, which they had of the gift of Eudo de Bordere, and grant of all the other lands which the fd. Adam might acquire, rendering 6;- a-year, and 2 marks for an obit.	Warburton, Woolfton, Northwich.	The brothers Alan, Philip and Mathew, chaplains, brother Hugh de Clayhyll, brother Rob. fitz Richard, Robert de Valencins, brother Rob. de Leſge, brother Alex. de Leſge, Angod the clerk.
1	75	No date.	Rich. Abbot of Kokerfont to Geoff. fitz Adam de Dutton. (Printed in His. Ches. I., 431.)	Re-grant of the lands which Adam gave the convent in Warburton, and other places, except 8 bovates [for which] the abbot and convent were to find a chaplain to minifter for the fouls of Adam, and the faithful departed.	Warburton.	Philip de Oreby, Gilbert de Limme, Rich. de —— Jord., Jordan the clerk.

A selection of Arley Charters appertaining to the Warburton family, from Arley Charters by William Beamont. Number sixty-eight is the charter by which Adam de Dutton was granted half of Warburton by Richard Fitz Alured when Adam married his daughter Agnes. The deed dated 1187 is the deed whereby Garnerus de Neapolis, prior of St John, granted Adam the other moiety of Warburton. The last deed, number seventy-five, gives back to Geoffrey de Dutton the land that Adam gave to the Canons of the Premonstratensian Order.

Warburton family coat of arms incorporates the chevron between three cormorants (Warburton) and the crest awarded to Sir Geoffrey Dutton, son of Adam, who fought in the Third Crusade under Richard of Cornwall. He returned in 1228 and was knighted for his efforts in the Holy Wars. The crest shows a Saracen's head with three ostrich plumes on a wreath.

Facsimile of the entry in the Domesday book showing that Ernwy held one of the manors of Warburton before the Norman Conquest. Ernwy also held Coddington and Alvanley. The Domesday entry is written in abbreviated Latin, and in rough translation it reads, 'This same William [son of Nigel] holds Warburton. Ernwy held it; he was free. [There is] half a hide paying tax, and land for one plough. There is 1 radman with 2 oxen. The value was 5 shillings; it is now worth 2 shillings'. The term 'radman' is sometimes translated as 'rider', and a 'hide' was a measurement of land. The value of the manor in the time of Edward the Confessor, before the Norman Conquest, is given first, and then the current value is shown dating from when the Domesday Book was compiled. In most cases in the north-west of England the value after the conquest was less than it had been previously.

Facsimile from the Domesday Book, showing Raven's possession of Warburton before the survey. Raven was a Saxon freeman. In free translation it reads, 'This same Osbern [son of Tezzo] also holds Warburton. Raven held it; he was a free man. [There is] half a hide which is taxable. Land for one plough. 1 radman, 2 villagers and 1 bordar with a half share in one plough'. The terms radman and bordar refer to different grades of villagers with different privileges and duties. Like the manor that Ernwy held, the value of Raven's manor had declined from 5s to 2s, with the added information in the Domesday entry that it was waste, meaning that it had perhaps been devastated during William's 'Harrying of the North'. Raven also held Dutton and Broxton.

Warburton Park. This hall was said to have been built by Sir Geoffrey de Warburton, grandson of Adam de Dutton, who settled in Warburton in 1248. There is little of the original building left. Park Farm House, which was built by R.E. Egerton Warburton, is said to contain one of the original walls of the old hall.

Arley Hall. The date of the original building of Arley Hall seems unclear. Ormerod states it to be 1469, whereas Norman Warburton declares it to be 1449. However, the hall and outbuildings were rebuilt by Sir Peter Arley when he succeeded his father in around 1648. The cruck barn and outbuildings of the estate date from that period but the present hall and chapel were rebuilt by Rowland Eyles Egerton Warburton (1804-91) between 1832 and 1845. Rowland was the high sheriff of Cheshire in 1833 and as also known as the blind poet of Cheshire.

ON PRESENTING A MIRROR

TO BE PLACED IN THE LADIES' CLOAK ROOM
AT KNUTSFORD, JAN. 14, 1857.

FAIR dancers, since the privilege is mine,
  A gift to place in that forbidden shrine,
Take, with the gift, the giver's caution too,
Gaze on yourselves as we shall gaze on you!
  While on your neck the circling jewels lie,
Dimm'd by the smile that sparkles in your eye,
While the fresh bouquet in your fingers held
Sees its own roses by your lips excell'd,
Ere with rash step ye mingle in the dance,
Fix on that mirror your observant glance;
May future ages see, reflected there,
Forms half so graceful, features half so fair!
  Let the prest glove cling closely to the hand,
Snap the gold clasp, the ivory fan expand,
Smooth the full skirt, adjust the pliant shoe,
Each point, each fold, fastidiously review.
So shall no rent the Brussels lace impair,
Though jealous pangs the inward bosom tear;
So shall the gown, through galop and quadrille,
Though hearts be crush'd, remain unruffled still.
  Go! partners wait impatient for the ball,
Go! smiling go! and bliss attend you all.

A poem from a book of poems and sonnets by R.E. Egerton Warburton printed in 1877. He also published a book of hunting songs in 1846.

Inscription in the front of a book of poems sent to the author's niece, the Hon. Rose Booth Wilbraham, who was the sister of the Earl of Latham. She lived at Blythe Hall in Latham

Eleven seals belonging to various members of the Warburton family.

From left to right, top row: Roger fitz Alured. The seal on the charter that granted half o Warburton to Adam de Dutton in around 1170.

Constable of Cheshire to Adam de Dutton, confirming the above charter, 1173.

Geoffrey de Dutton, son of Adam. This Geoffrey joined the Crusades and went to the Hol Land with John de Lacy. He was successful and was granted a crest of a Saracen's head Laurence Bostock wrote in 1572: 'This Galfrid [Geoffrey] lived 1244. He was serving his Prync and vanquished a Sarrazion in combate.' The principle mansion of this Geoffrey was at Suttor He died in around 1248.

Middle row: Petrus de Dutton (living 1261). Petrus was the grandson of Geoffrey de Dutton He assumed the name of Warburton.

Geoffrey de Warburton (senior). Succeeded his father in around 1343. He was seneschal o Trafford and Stoney Dunham.

Sir Geoffrey de Warburton (junior) He was living in 1381 and had children called Geoffrey Thomas, John and Katherine. In 1338 a marriage was entered into between his son Geoffre and Nicola, the daughter of Sir John Danyers. The Warburton estates were to be settled on th male heirs of this marriage, but both Geoffrey and Thomas died without male issue. Seals five and six are from the same charter, namely that on the contract of marriage between Geoffrey and Nicola.

John, son of Geoffrey de Warburton junior. He did not hold the seat of Warburton for long. He succeeded to his father's estates in or before 1383 and died probably in 1384-85, leaving a son, Peter, who was only thirteen. Sir John Massey of Tatton had wardship of Peter and he contracted him to marry his daughter, Dulcie. This marriage did take place but was unsuccessful and the couple later divorced.

Bottom row: Peter de Warburton. This seal is from the charter dated 28 June 1412 between Peter de Warburton and William le Spencer granting the latter the manor of Warburton. Peter fought in the battle of Shrewsbury on the side of Henry Percy in the 1403 rebellion. He also fought at Agincourt. He died in around 1420.

Sir Geoffrey Warburton. This seal is dated 8 Henry V, which was the date of his father's death (1421 – the eighth year of Henry V's reign).

Sir Geoffrey Warburton. He was in possession of the estates as early as 1429. In a deed dated the same, William Percival of Budworth refers to him as Lord of Warburton. This deed is witnessed by the Duke of Gloucester, the King's cousin, and releases Percival's right and claim to Budworth to Geoffrey Warburton. He died in around 1448 and was succeeded by his son, Piers (Wise Piers), who built Arley Hall.

Sir Peter Warburton. The dissolution of monasteries took place in this Peter's time. He died in 1553.

Peter Egerton Warburton (1813-89). Peter Egerton Warburton was the son of Revd Roland Egerton and his wife, Emma Croxton. Emma changed her name to Warburton when she became heiress to her uncle, Sir Peter Warburton of Arley. Peter joined the army in 1831 and led the life of an adventurer from then on.

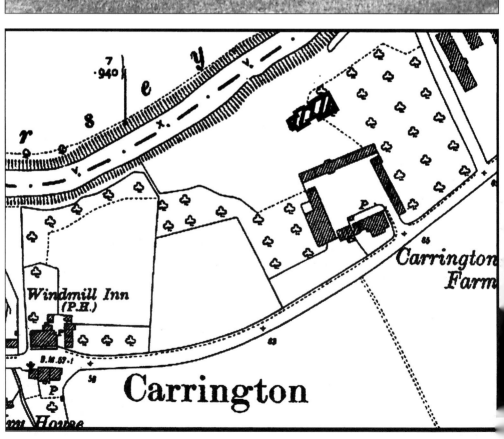

Opposite top: Carrington Hall Farm was built sometime during the mid-1800s. It was a fine brick building with several outbuildings and included over 258 acres of farmland. In 1889 the hall farm was almost destroyed by fire when children that were playing in the hay barn managed to set it alight. The fire brigade, who were stationed at Sale, were called out but by the time they arrived, the villagers of Carrington had brought the fire under control. The last tenant of the farm was a Mr Tom Bradbury-Mayer, who was at one time chairman of Carrington Parish Council. He farmed the estate for over twenty-seven years until the hall was demolished during the 1950s.

Bottom: This extract from the Ordnance Survey map of 1908 shows the exact location of Carrington Hall in relation to Carrington Hall Farm. The position of Carrington Hall was much closer to the river Mersey than that of the Hall Farm. Carrington Hall is the shaded rectangular building at the top of the picture, while the farm and outbuildings are the large square buildings situated closer to the road. To achieve this information, the Tithe map of Carrington, dated 1838, has been overlaid onto the Ordnance Survey map of 1908 to give the appearance of the two buildings being in existence at the same time. In 1942, Kelly's street directory noted that 'a barn in the parish retains an old oak carved beam, bearing the arms of the Carrington family in good preservation'.

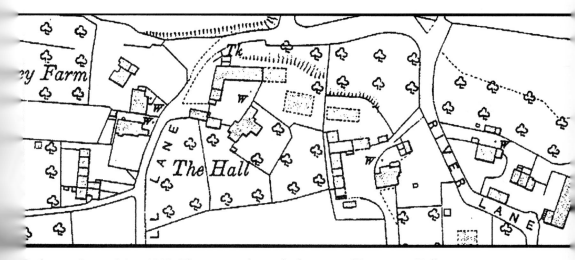

Ordnance Survey Map, 1907. This extract shows the location of Partington Hall.

Mill Bank, Partington, was once the home of the Occleston family. This family was not of noble descent but amassed wealth from their business undertakings. Thomas Occleston built the paper mill in Partington in the early nineteenth century

Three

Village Life

The village of Warburton, as we have seen in previous chapters, has a long history. There are even dinosaur footprints on one of the sandstone slabs used as fencing! There have been fragments of Romano-British pottery found in the Moss Brow area of Warburton and flints identified as Neolithic or early Bronze Age found near the mill site. There is also evidence of round barrows, or burial grounds, in Warburton. This indicates some sort of settlement in the area well before the village proper was established. These burial grounds served as some protection for the ancestors of the dead buried within them, so the settlements tended to be situated close to the mounds.

'Weard byrig' or Warburton is believed by some to have been originally established as one of fourteen forts erected by Queen Aethelflaed along the boundary between Mercia and Northumbria to protect her land from the Danish invaders, although there seems to be some doubt about this attribution. It is thought the fort was built in around AD 915. The first time 'Warburton' is referred to is in AD 991, when the village paid ten Anglo-Saxon shillings in Danegeld to keep the Danes out of Mercia. This would be the equivalent of £50 in modern currency and was a considerable amount, signifying that Warburton was a fairly important place.

However, Warburton was very isolated, with the moss on one side and the river Mersey on the other. The road from Lymm crossed a ford at the mill, went up to Wigsey Lane and then back over the river to Lancashire. This was the only road until Bent Lane was cut in 1637 by Richard Drinkwater of Bent Farm. Gates were erected at either end of the lane to try and preserve it as a private thoroughfare for the Drinkwater family, but as this road was a much easier and more straightforward way out of the village, the townsfolk resented not being able to use it, and eventually the matter came to court in Knutsford in 1735. There is no record of the result of this action, but the road must have eventually become a public right of way. The villagers were obliged to keep the roads of Warburton in good repair. A day was chosen when all the required men came out together, each holding having to provide one man and a shovel. Fines were incurred if anyone failed in their duty.

In Anglo-Saxon times Warburton was already settled. The Domesday book or survey, completed by William the Conqueror's men after the Norman Conquest, says that Warburton consisted of two manors held by freemen Ernwy and Raven. However, the land in and around Warburton is described as waste in the survey, meaning, in this context, land that has been destroyed after the Conquest in an attempt to take control of the north. We do not know for certain where the two manors were, although it is generally assumed that one of them was on the site of Warburton Park Hall. The population of the two manors, again taken from the Domesday survey, was approximately thirty-five people. Although this seems a small number, it was fairly average for medieval times. Eventually the two manors became one and the Warburton family made its seat there.

The village of Warburton remained untouched to a certain degree throughout these changes although the feudal system was stricter under the Normans than it had been in Anglo-Saxon times. The strip cultivation of the land that was established by the Anglo-Saxons endured through to Norman times and beyond. In fact, some villagers' strips can still be seen in Warburton.

The feudal system meant that most of the villagers owed allegiance to the lord of the manor and had to do some work on his land. The village community shared in the cultivation of the land in and around the village, and each had a share in the meadow, which lay near the village, and on which they could graze their animals. However, the lot of the villeins who were inextricably tied to their lords, was not an easy one. They were not free to leave and had few rights. They would also be expected to fight for their masters if the time came.

The Warburton family remained at Warburton until 1469, when they moved to Arley Hall, leaving a bailiff to organize the affairs of the village and act as a link between the Warburtons who remained in Warburton and the main family at Arley. The most famous of these bailiffs was Arnold Drinkwater, who left diaries that are still preserved at the Cheshire record office, from which we get some interesting information about Warburton and the lives of its occupants. The volumes are small and the writing even smaller but he must have been a very organized and conscientious man. The Court Leet procedures are noted under various headings such as felons, burglary and robbery, and in around 1739 he writes that 'every householder keeping a team and every cottager and laborer in the parish and being no hire servant by the year shall work on the Highway. No women or children are to be sent'.

Another source of information in later years comes from the census and directories. We can see in the directories of Cheshire that although the main Warburton family had removed to Arley Hall, it remained the sole landowner and retained the lordship of the manor. The directories also tell us some basic facts about the village. For example, in 1864 the incumbent of the church was Revd Daniel Beaumont, who supported the schools and charities, and the annual value of his living and the rectory was £250. The population was 482, and the landlord of the Saracen's Head was James Langton, who was also a wheelwright and farmer. There was an extensive flourmill that was owned by Mr William Shaw. It was powered by the water of the river Bollin, which flowed into the Mersey. John Stubbs was the stationmaster and Peter Ramsdale was the shopkeeper. The sub-postmaster was Samuel Williamson and letters were supposed to arrive at 8.30 a.m.

The family became known as Egerton Warburton when Emma, sole heir of her father Sir Peter Warburton, married Rowland Egerton, and they remained the sole landowners and the lord and lady of the manor until the death of Captain John Egerton Warburton. In 1918 the Warburton estate was sold to the Co-operative Wholesale Society Ltd, although the 1923 Directory of Cheshire tells us that the landowners in Warburton were the trustees of Captain John Egerton Warburton, not the Co-operative Society.

In earlier days Warburton was a fief of the priory of St John of Jerusalem and as such was beyond the reach of the law. There is a legend that Dick Turpin found sanctuary in a secret room at the Saracen's Head. A room was indeed found in the inn when renovations were being carried out in the nineteenth century. It contains armour that is now lodged at Arley Hall. Until as late as 1868 the residents of Warburton were exempt from jury service and under the jurisdiction of their own Court Leet, which was held at the Saracen's Head every November. In his diaries, Arnold Drinkwater writes notes on the procedures of the Court Leet, which was allowed to make many of its own laws. Warburton had a constable as early as 1720. In the town books can be found lists of constables, their wages and accounts. Warburton would be under the jurisdiction of the petty sessions in Bucklow Hundred where the constables would appear together with their offenders. The stocks can still be seen in Warburton. They were placed in their present position by Mr Bariff, the landlord of the Saracen's Head, in 1900.

The church was responsible for the building of the first school in Warburton. The school was built on land belonging to Mr R.E. Egerton Warburton in 1832, at a cost of £160. The money used was partly from the Clothing Charity and partly from parish funds. The church paid £3 16s per year together with the collections from the Sunday services. Mr Egerton Warburton built a new school in

872 and eventually the old school became a cottage.

A 1601 act stated that overseers of the poor should be appointed in each parish to raise money by taxation for the relief of that parish's poor. Relief of the poor in Warburton seems to have been quite generous. The parish was responsible both for the poor in its own parish and for those who had been born in Warburton but moved away. The 1860 Directory of Cheshire states that Sarah Drinkwater gave by her will the sum of £60, and in 1810 John Leigh gave the sum of £10. The money was to be distributed annually, around Christmas, to clothe the poor. Thus the Clothing Charity was set up to provide blankets clothing, medical care etc. The township books give detailed accounts of how the money was spent and on whom. The Clothing Charity was passed over to the Charities Commissioners in 1890.

So we have a picture of a pretty Cheshire village clustered mostly round the old church and surrounded by thriving farms and fields of crops, which still lives on today to some extent, although we do not have the all-powerful lord of the manor who ruled so much of the life of the village. The remains of the village cross can be found at the junction of Wigsey Lane and Townfield Lane, together with the stocks, and one can imagine traders and merchants doing business there in days gone by. The cottages have lost their thatches, most being replaced by tiles, but Warburton retains its air of history, and echoes with the ghosts of times gone by.

The village of Carrington is situated about eight and a half miles south of Manchester between Sale and Partington, and is bordered by the river Mersey. Prior to local government reorganization in 1974 it was in Cheshire, but since then has been part of the Metropolitan Borough of Trafford. The origins of Carrington can be traced back to the late eleventh century when Hamo de Carrington was granted a manor in Bowdon, although there may have been some settlement in the area much earlier. The village, however, was not mentioned in the Domesday survey of 1086 so probably developed over a longer period, sometime after this date.

The houses and farms that gradually sprang up around the manor hall, and were eventually to form the nucleus of the village, developed on either side of the main highway that ran between Sale and Partington. This type of layout gave the village the appearance of being divided into two halves, but was a feature often seen in English villages and is commonly known as a street village. Many villages in England were built close to or around the parish church; Carrington was not, however, and did not have a church of its own until 1757-59, when St George's was built.

Carrington was in the parish of Bowdon and was not made a parish in its own right until 1887. This meant that the villagers of Carrington had to travel to St Mary's in Bowdon, St Martin's in Ashton upon Mersey or St Michael's in Flixton to attend church services. The church of St Mary in Bowdon has a chapel dedicated to the Carrington family. The parish registers for St Mary's, Bowdon, and St Michael's in Flixton provide us with information on many of the families who lived in the village of Carrington. One example is the Millat family who lived in Carrington and attended St Michael's church in Flixton. The parish registers for 1636 and 1641 chronicle some of the major events in their lives:

'May 8th 1636 the baptism of Anne daughter of Hamnett (Hamlett) Millat (t) of Carrington.
January 13th 1641 the burial of Anne Millatt daughter of Hamlet Millett of Carrington
April 19th 1641 the burial Hamlett Millett of Carrington.'

Although sources of information such as parish records and assorted deeds and documents provide us with a small amount of information, they are few in number and we really know very little about the village until the late eighteenth century, from which time more records are available for research.

A journal stated in 1758 that 'The Honorable Earl of Warrington has given an acre of land in Carrington Township on which to erect and build a chapel of ease, a house for a clergyman to live in and a school house and also a thousand guineas towards the building of the same'. The church of St George was built in 1759 and the adjoining school in 1833. The Stamford family and residents of Carrington Hall were fortunate enough to have their own private pews in the church, whereas many of the villagers rented them. In 1759 the annual price of a pew ranged from three to six shillings. Mrs Arstinghall paid six shillings while Thomas Yates paid only three shillings. The first baptismal entry for St George's was for Elizabeth, daughter of John and Martha Meat, on 9 September 1759, and the first burial was William, son of Thomas and Alice Yates of Carrington, 24 February 1760. The church was still in use until its closure in 1990. It is now a listed building but remains closed; the vicarage is used as a garden centre and the school as a private business.

In 1779 Bishop Porteus reported: 'Carrington village consisted of sixty houses, twelve of which were Presbyterians, one Presbyterian meetinghouse and no papists.' The Tithe map and the census of Carrington, both dated 1841, give us our first real glimpse of how the village would have appeared, and some idea of the type of people who lived there. The village was mostly made up of farms and houses scattered around the manor hall, with the surrounding land used for agriculture. The Tithe map listed the hall as Carrington Hall and Pleasure Gardens; it included a kitchen garden, an orchard and a farmyard with buildings. The village also had a dam and a mill, which was powered by a water wheel.

In total area Carrington covered 2091 acres, which consisted of 476 acres of arable land, 782 acres of meadow and pasture, 12 acres of woodland and 749 acres of moss land. The Tithe apportionment of 1838, which accompanied the Tithe map, lists some of the Tithes, which had to be paid as a form of rent. These included: one penny for every old stock of bees; three pence for five geese; two pence for every person exercising a trade; and one penny for every garden. The census for 1841 lists the village as a whole, with very few references to individual buildings. However, one building which was listed by name was Maypole House, the home of Peter Hollinworth, a farmer. Maypole House was probably where the village maypole was originally sited. The custom of dancing around the maypole, though now long gone, was once a common feature of village life.

The occupants of the village were equipped with a range of skills that enabled them to be self-sufficient, a necessary feature of rural life when transport was difficult and villages were often isolated. The village had its own mill to grind corn, a dam, a blacksmith and three providers of groceries and sundries. Slater's directory of 1848 lists the following occupants:

William Ikin – Miller, Carrington Mill
Jane Howard – Schoolmistress, National School
Elizabeth Blinston – Blacksmith and Farrier and Dealer in Groceries and Sundries
John Robinson, Peter Daine and Elizabeth Crampton – Shopkeepers and Dealer in Groceries
Henry Daine – Windmill Inn
Thomas Moore – Blue Bell Inn
John Wright – Tailor
Joseph Occleston – Boot Maker
Samuel Burgess – Basket Maker
Mr William Walkden of Carrington Hall, Revd George Heron, Mr Thomas Unsworth – Nobility and Gentry

Although the village was only small, it had two inns, the Windmill Inn and the Blue Bell Inn. The Windmill Inn was used as a venue for the Court Baron, which was held twice a year. The Court Baron dealt with matters ranging from the repair of hedges and stiles to the upkeep of roads and farm buildings. The Blue Bell Inn was situated close to where the Millhouse Café is today, and would have stood opposite the dam. On the Tithe map it is listed as the Bell Inn and yard. There is a story that 'One day, the Blue Bell sank into the earth and disappeared'. Although this may sound far fetched there may be an element of truth in it, as the high level of water in the area could have caused the pub to subside thus giving the appearance of sinking.

Carrington is situated on low-lying ground close to the river Mersey and during the winter months was often flooded. To control this and also to provide an irrigation system, sluices were built at intervals from the river to control the water flow. Many of the old field names refer to the connection with water and include names such as Amsterdam, Milldam and Dam field. There was a bridge over the river Mersey that connected Carrington to the village of Flixton. It was situated close to Carrington Hall and legend has it that it was a Lady Carrington who was responsible for building the bridge. In 1746, an order for the repair of footbridges described the bridge as 'a wooden footbridge only, carts had to use the ford'. The bridge linked up to a footpath, then called Carrington Lane, which ran along the side of the river Mersey into Flixton. In 1840 the wooden bridge was replaced with an iron one, which was much wider and could take both pedestrians and carts. The bridge can be seen clearly marked on the Ordnance Survey map of 1842 and continues to be shown as late as 1928. It gradually fell into disrepair and was eventually demolished. The Irlam steel works bought the scrap iron and melted it down to be reused. In 1907 a stone bridge was built over the river Mersey at Flixton and also a new connecting road between Carrington and Flixton. The new road, Carrington Road, was a very straight road, which has since become known locally as the Mile Road, although it is less than a mile in length.

In August 1887 the *Chronicle* newspaper reported: 'This fruitful village has a very antique and picturesque appearance; so much so that landscape sketchers are frequently visiting it to sketch some of the old picturesque buildings and scenery of the place. Daine's farm is a place of such note and has been in the occupation of the Daines for 500 years. It is now in the occupation of Mr John Collins a nephew of the last surviving Daine who occupied the farm. On the farm is an old pear tree supposed to be planted some 300 to 400 years ago. In the centre of the village from 30 to 40 years ago, a corn mill stood on the road from Ashton to Partington with a hold of water to the extent of upwards of one Cheshire acre. It was known by the name of Carrington Mill Dam and at one time abounded with fish of various kinds. Fifty years ago handloom weaving was the staple trade in Carrington.'

As far back as 1914, concern was raised over the effect industrialization was having on the area. In that year the Reverend Digby Walsh of St George's church in Carrington wrote in a letter, 'the neighbourhood is deteriorating. Very large works (the Partington Steel Works) have been built during the past two years within a mile from the house and a large soda works are in the process of construction at about the same distance: all the oak and ash trees are dying'.

The appearance of the village has altered considerably since the 1940s and the development of the chemical industry. Many of the original farms and houses have now disappeared and only a few of them still remain. There have been some new housing developments in the form of council houses, which were built during the late 1940s and 1960s but very little in the way of private housing. In 2001 however, a small new housing development has been undertaken using land situated close to the Millhouse Café. In recent years Carrington has been brought onto the world stage and become the focus of media attention with the development of the new football training grounds for both Manchester United and Manchester City.

Carrington Moss was originally around a thousand acres in total and probably began life as a lake during the end of the ice age, and over a long period of time gradually developed into swampland before finally turning into moss. The moss has been instrumental in the way that Carrington and the surrounding area developed, as it would have been a valuable source of food such as game, while also providing fuel in the form of peat. During the latter part of the nineteenth century a small area of the moss was reclaimed as a result of the construction of the Cheshire Lines railway in 1873, but it was in 1880 that the reclamation began in earnest when Manchester City Council bought the moss from the trustees of the late Earl of Stamford for £38,000.

The problem of waste disposal in the city of Manchester was acute and Carrington Moss presented the authority with an ideal opportunity to solve the problem of disposing with the ever-increasing amount of night soil from the city centre. The moss was large enough to provide an adequate dumping ground far away from the city, in an area that was not heavily populated. The waste was transported from the city of Manchester by boat along the Irwell and the Mersey and, after 1894, the Manchester Ship Canal. The night soil would then be distributed evenly over the moss and after a suitable period, the land would be improved agriculturally. In order to do this a central road system was constructed that allowed for the easy transport of the waste, while a narrow gauge railway was specially constructed to distribute the waste over the moss. The railway covered an area of six miles and at one time employed between 120 and 150 workmen.

After the land had been left for about one year it was deeply dug over and potatoes and other crops were planted in rotation. The Health Committee decided that as the land became available for agricultural use it was to be let out. It was divided into rectangular fields, which were then rented out to farmers. The first tenancies were let in 1887, and by 1889 all the land had been taken. The venture was a complete success for Manchester City Council, who between the years 1886-89 made a return of £61,022 against expenditure of £123,818. In 1903 T. Alfred Coward wrote in his book *Picturesque Cheshire*, 'Carrington Moss– was once a mass of purple ling with bell heather and silky cotton grass – grouse was plentiful – Short eared owl reared young in the open. Vipers were common'. By 1938 the Manchester Corporation decided they had no further use for it and the land was sold to Petrocarbon Ltd.

Partington village is situated about eleven miles south of Manchester, between Warburton and Carrington. Prior to the local government reorganization in 1974, the village was in Cheshire, but today it is administered by the Metropolitan Borough of Trafford. Partington was at one time separated from Lancashire by the river Mersey, which ran along its border, but in 1894 when the Manchester Ship Canal was built, the river at this point was diverted into it and a large section was widened to form Partington coaling basin.

The early history of Partington could possibly be traced back as far as the Anglo-Saxon period, as there may have been some early settlement in the area. 'Ton' is an Anglo-Saxon word for farm, and legend has it that a Viking by the name of Cythric Silkybeard led a party of Vikings along the river Mersey to Partington, where he and his men killed around twenty of the Partington villagers. As place names are often a reliable source for dating towns and villages there may be some truth in this, as Partington is referred to in *Place Names of Cheshire* as a farm associated with a man called Pearta. Although Partington was omitted from the Domesday Survey of 1086, a small settlement may have already been established in the area which was not recorded in the survey. The first written evidence for the village of Partington appears in the year 1260, during the reign of Henry III, when a family who lived in the area took the name of Partington as its own: De Henri de Partington.

Partington was originally part of the ancient fee of the Massey family of Dunham Massey, and was governed by the Court Leet of Dunham Massey. During the reign of Edward I, Hamon de Massey, who was lord of the manor, rented out large portions of his estate; this included the village of Partington.

The village was around 800 acres in total and was considerably smaller, both in size and importance, than its neighbour Carrington, which had a total acreage of over 2019. By the year 1666 Partington had been rented out to the following people: 1. George Lord Delamere of Dunham Massey was lord of a third part of Partington, which had originally been held by the Carrington family of Carrington, and was also chief lord of two other parts that were originally held by the barons of Dunham Massey; 2. John Hadfield of Over-Cliffe, in the county of Derby had a sixth part of Partington according to the original deed made by Hamon de Massey; 3. Thomas Warburton of Partington had another sixth part of Partington, along with an eighteenth part of a further sixth part; 4. John Warburton of Partington and John Owen of Partington each had a sixth part of Partington for the payment of one penny in lieu of a pair of gloves; 5. John Partington of Partington had two parts of a third of a sixth part of Partington. This may appear complicated, but in simple terms meant that the lord of the manor owned the land, then sub-let the whole of the village of Partington to various tenants.

The early history of Partington can be traced through old deeds and documents, and it is probably accurate to say that it was a quiet, rural village consisting mainly of small scattered farms. The soil in the area was rich in peat, suitable for growing wheat, barley, oats and hay, and most of the villagers earned their living off the land.

The people who lived in and around the village were all tenants of the Dunham Massey estate, and the estate papers, which survive today, are a valuable source of information as to how the village was run. Quarter Sessions records are concerned with law and order, and one of these early records, taken from the Quarter Sessions held in 1705, refers to an accusation of witchcraft which took place in the village of Partington in Cheshire. A woman known as Jane Whitall, of Partington, took some whey to the house of Susannah Holt, also of Partington. Susannah Holt said to Jane, 'thou dirty Quean get out of my house, thou keeps my son from me all night and I in this condition, but I will plague thee'.

About three days after this, Jane Whitall was seized with blindness and later suffered a type of fit. Jane said: 'I saw Susannah Holt stand before me at the fire side with her staff in her hand in Edmond Erloms house in Partington, after which I was seized with a pain in my right side and sweated very much and thought I had a mighty weight laid upon my legs, whilst the pain in my side ceased.' The pains and the blindness continued for a further few days until Jane Whitall sent for Susannah Holt. When she arrived, Jane Whitall punched Susannah Holt on the nose and made it bleed. This aggressive action solved the problem, because from that moment, Jane was free from pain and the blindness disappeared. Susannah Holt was duly charged and appeared at the following Quarter Sessions, with the result that she was bound over to the sum of £40 for good behaviour.

As the nineteenth century progressed there was a gradual increase in the population of Partington, from 457 in 1841 to 587 by 1901. This small rise, in an otherwise rural farming community, may have been due to the increase in industrial activity that was occurring throughout England at the time, but can also be attributed to the construction of the Manchester Ship Canal, as labourers who were looking for work were attracted to the area. Transport links to the rest of the country were also improved when the Cheshire Lines Railway constructed a rail link between Broadheath and Warrington in 1873, resulting in the village of Partington having a railway station of its own.

The nineteenth-century census information is useful for providing information on the people who lived in and around the village, but unfortunately the early ones for 1841 and 1851 do not refer to many of the buildings by name. Slater's street directory for 1848, however, provides us with a list of the types of business that were a part of everyday life, and with this information we can begin to build a picture of how the village would have appeared:

William Lucas – Blacksmith and Farrier
Isaac Smith – Boot maker
Allen Pollard – Boot maker
Thomas Hesketh – Corn dealer
John Pitt – Sadler and landlord of the William IV
George Pollard – Shopkeeper and dealer in groceries and sundries
Robert Whitelegg – Shopkeeper and dealer in groceries and sundries
William Clarke – Greyhound
Thomas Winstanley – Carpenter and Builder

From this list it can be seen that Partington, like most isolated rural communities, was self-sufficient, although the village did have direct contact with both Carrington and Warburton, both of which were within easy walking distance. Many of the village children would have attended the school in Carrington, which had been paid for by the Earl of Stamford, and it is also interesting to note that some of the family names mentioned in the list of occupants still have descendants living in Partington today.

Road names such as Chapel Lane and Moss Lane started to appear in 1851, while Lock Lane, Warburton Lane, River Lane, Hall Lane, and Scroggins Lane appeared about thirty years later, in 1881. The nucleus of the village was centered on the village green, which was situated close to Partington Hall. By 1851 the village was made up of ninety-three houses. The village stocks, which were used as an ancient form of punishment, were situated at the junction of Chapel Lane and Wood Lane.

Partington did not have its own church until the church of St Mary the Virgin was built in 1884. The cost of the church was £3,500, with the money provided jointly by the Revd Heron and Sir William Cunliffe Brooks, who had purchased a third of the land from Lord Stamford in 1858. In 1885 Partington was made a parish in its own right; prior to this the villagers had had to use St George's church in Carrington or St Mary's in Bowdon. The new church, designed by Mr G. Truefitt of Bloomsbury Square, London, was built of Runcorn stone in the Gothic style. There was, however, a strong non-conformist following in both Partington and Carrington, and the earliest of their churches, the United Reformed church, was built in 1714, while the Wesleyan chapel was founded in 1843 and rebuilt in 1861.

The village remained relatively unchanged until the 1950s, although the population rose slowly to 957. Between the years 1951 and 1961 the village underwent a sharp increase in population to around 6,574 inhabitants. This rapid increase was the direct result of a plan put forward by Bucklow Rural District Council to transform the village of Partington into a 'Model' town, hoping to increase the population to around 6,000. Over 800 houses were constructed, the first ten being completed by December 1952. A new sewage disposal system costing over £170,000 had to be built to accommodate the sudden rise in population. The new houses were to provide homes for overspill tenants from Manchester, Salford and Stretford, as well as providing additional houses for the local residents of Partington. This housing project changed the face of Partington completely and transformed what was once a quiet, rural, farming village into a small town.

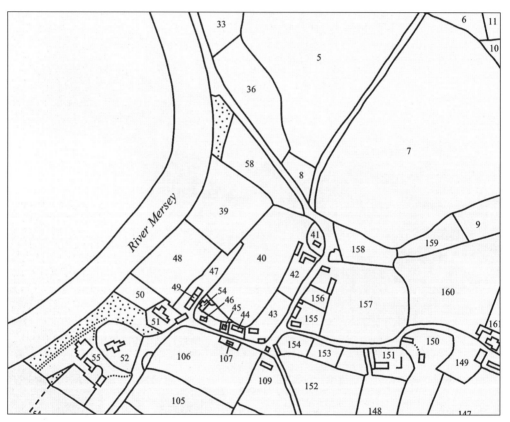

Warburton Tithe Map, 1834. Tithes were originally a payment of one tenth of the produce of the land to the monasteries, or later the churches, to help support them. In later years Tithes were sold, so the Tithes could end up being paid to a layman landowner. This system became defunct as it did nor encourage farmers to develop their farms, as they knew that an amount of their produce would not be their own. There was also some resentment that the money, as it eventually became, was not going to the church as was its initial purpose, but to line the pockets of the great landowners. The Tithe map is accompanied by an apportionment to which the numbers on the map apply. The apportionment shows who owned the piece of land, who occupied it and how much the Tithe was. It is a useful tool when researching the history of the area, particularly when used in conjunction with the census, as it shows us exactly where the property lay and what kind of property it was, giving us a fuller picture of the area and the people living there.

Warburton village *c*. 1908. Notice the sandstone slabs that make up the fences to the property. This photograph was taken from by the stocks and shows the old cottages, one of which was formerly Warburton School.

The Pipe and Punch Bowl. This photograph was taken from the graveyard of the old church in Warburton. It can be seen on the Tithe map that part of the row of cottages adjacent to the church was at one time a public house. The landowner was Rowland Eyres Egerton Warburton and the occupier, whom we can assume to have been the landlord, was Thomas Tittle, who was married to William Warburton's daughter Sarah at Warburton church in 1830. The inn was converted into cottages in the eighteenth century and the cellars beneath filled in.

The post office at Warburton. The post office was designed by John Douglas, who was a famous architect. He was also responsible for the designs of the new church, the school and the parish hall. In 1878 the post-mistress was Mrs Mary Williamson, and letters came through Warrington to arrive at 9.30 a.m.

The new school at Warburton. This school was built in 1872 by R.E. Egerton Warburton, having been designed by John Douglas.

The old school at Warburton. The school was built in the 1830s on land belonging to Mr R.E. Egerton Warburton at a cost of £160, £70 of which came from the Clothing Charity and £90 from the parish. One feature was a block of stone over the window at the gable end, in which was carved 'The fear of the Lord is the beginning of wisdom'. When the new school was built in 1872 this old building was used as a Sunday school for which the church paid £3 16s 0d a year. In 1891 the school was turned into a cottage, as the Sunday school had been transferred to the Parish Room at Moss Brow.

The Saracen's Head. Geoffrey, son of Adam de Dutton so excelled himself in the Crusades in the thirteenth century that he was awarded a crest in the form of a Saracen's head to add to the family coat of arms. The crest can be seen over the doorway of the present building. Arthur Barff was the landlord in the 1896 Directory of Cheshire.

Warburton Park Farm. There are no remains of the manor house that was once the main residence of the Dutton family, but it is assumed to have been on the site where the farm now stands. The family changed their name from Dutton to Warburton in the thirteenth century when Peter, son of Geoffrey Dutton, took the name. The hall was most likely moated.

Warburton Cross and stocks The stocks were retrieved from the wall of a cottage on the green and a field gatepost, where they had been usefully employed. They were put in their present position in 1900 by Mr Barff, the landlord of the Saracen's Head, with the permission of Mr Warburton. The wooden planking was replaced at this time. It can be seen on this photograph that the stumps have been broken and straps are securing them. The base and steps of the cross, which are all that remain, are made of blocks of local sandstone. The cross itself is missing but it can be seen where it would fit into the base.

Village crosses provided a meeting place for merchants and tradesmen. In the time of the plague a bowl of vinegar was placed at the base of the cross and any money to be exchanged was placed in the bowl to purify it. There was such a plague in Lymm in 1652 and 1653 and maybe the cross at Warburton was used for this purpose. On the Tithe map of 1839 a marking can be seen at the junction of Townfield, Church Green and Paddock Lane, which is most likely the original position of the cross. There is a also a well marked on the 1966 OS map of Warburton near to where the cross lies now.

The barn at Moss Brow Farm. This farm is one of the five largest in Warburton with between eighty and ninety acres, currently farmed by Mr Clegg. The other large farms are Carr Green with around 100 acres, Birch Farm with eighty to ninety acres, Park Farm with 300 acres and the Bent with around 100 acres. A barbed early Bronze-Age arrowhead and a shard of Romano-British pottery were found on this site.

Archaeological investigations at Moss Brow Farm, 1999. Photo courtesy of Dr M. Nevell.

The Bent. This photograph shows the barn at the back of Bent Farm. The Drinkwater family built it in 1600, about the same time as the farmhouse. The Drinkwaters often held the post of bailiff for the Warburton family and built Bent Lane in 1637 to provide a more direct route to Lymm. Although this barn is not a cruck barn, we can see two cruck blades with a tie beam going across, joined by two wall plates. The barn has been converted from a threshing barn to a shippon, which was common in the late eighteenth century and early nineteenth century. The farm, which is reputed to be the oldest house in Warburton, is a half-timbered structure that was renovated in 1877.

Birch Farm is situated on Moss Road, Warburton. It is of particular interest because of its cruck barn. It is on the 1757 Warburton estate map and is mentioned on the 1778 rental as 'two dwelling houses, orchard and barn'.

Wigsey Farm, Warburton. This farm is situated on Paddock Lane and comprises the farmhouse, the shippon, a brick hay barn and two steel-framed barns. The farm had has several phases of development, one of which shows how the farm changed from arable to dairy farming at the time of the industrial revolution. The earliest mention of Wigsey Farm is on the Warburton estate map of 1757, which is part of the Charles Foster collection at Arley Hall. There are two seventeenth-century cruck buildings on the site – the farmhouse and the L-shaped shippon. It would seem that the remains of the cruck building in the latter predate those of the crucks in the farmhouse. This type of timber building consists of cruck blades that form the frame and roof of the building in one. The crucks are split from the same tree and tapered to form the arch. There are two types of cruck. This example is a raised cruck, which means the cruck blades sit on a sandstone wall. In the other type of cruck the blades rise straight from the floor.

Carr Green Farm, situated on Carr Green Lane between Lower Carr Green Farm and Higher Carr Green Farm.

Paddocklane Farm, situated on Paddock Lane opposite Paddock Lake Farm. It is currently undergoing renovation work. The farm is on the Tithe map of 1834.

Onion Farm. This farm is a grade two listed building and lies together with Villa Farm, a stable block and hay barn to the east of Warburton Park. This farm is the earliest known vernacular building in Trafford and as such is of great importance. The farm was investigated by the University of Manchester Archaeological Unit, which identified various stages of renovation. It is thought to have been built in the early sixteenth century and was originally timber framed, but had several additions – including the building of a second floor – in the eighteenth century. Of particular interest is a wall painting on the ground floor. Although these wall paintings were common in the sixteenth century, few have survived in Greater Manchester. This particular painting shows a female figure with what is believed to be a goose on her right hand. There is a second figure, probably a man, and a Tudor rose. Dr Mike Nevell has given a detailed description of the painting in *Archaeology of Trafford*. The existence of this painting could denote that the occupant was of greater standing than a yeoman farmer. However, we have no evidence of this.

The newly built farmhouse at Paddocklane Farm, photographed in 2001.

Parkgate Farm. This farm lies, as its name suggests, at the start of Park Road, presumably where the gates to Warburton Hall stood.

Brook House Farm, Warburton Lane. You can see the end of the original farmhouse on the left, with Brook House in the centre.

Rebuilding at Paddocklake Farm. The plate above the door shows the date 1717.

Matchington Farm, on Sawpit Street. It lies on the border with Dunham Massey.

The Beeches. This house is situated at the junction of Dunham Road and Warburton Lane.

Rose and Lilac Cottage. This quaint little cottage stands almost opposite Onion Farm.

Cottages as they are today in Warburton village. The first one is marked number forty-nine on the Tithe map, where the occupier is listed as John Hampden and his entry comprises house, barn and yard.

Cottage next to what was the old school building near Warburton old church, photographed in 2001. The cottage has been extended and re-thatched.

Cottage in Warburton village. It is listed on the Tithe map as number forty-six. Mary, Martha and Jane Hamnett lived here in 1939. We can see the old schoolhouse next door.

Townfield House at the crossroads of Paddock Lane and Townfield Lane. The name Townfield may derive from the old medieval farming system.

Holly Cottage on Dunham Road.

Carrington Bridge, Carrington. Legend has it that it was a Lady Carrington who was responsible for building a bridge across the river Mersey. The iron bridge seen in the photograph was built around 1840 and replaced an earlier wooden structure, which linked Carrington to Flixton. Although the iron bridge was only wide enough to take a horse and cart, it provided a vital link across the river Mersey. Carrington Parish Council reported on 1 May 1895 that the bridge was in a dangerous condition. They appointed a committee to solicit voluntary subscriptions for the necessary work to be undertaken. The estimated sum required for this repair was £50. In 1907, Flixton Bridge was opened and the iron bridge gradually became redundant, as people used the stone bridge and the new straight road into Carrington. The iron bridge eventually fell into disrepair and was demolished.

The Cross Cottage. This cottage is situated next to the village cross and stocks, hence its name. The cross and stocks were originally located a short distance away before they were moved to their present location.

Carrington Road in the 1950s. Carrington Road, which is also known locally as the Mile Road, has a long history of flooding during the winter months. Despite attempts to overcome the problem, including the building of Sale Water Park, the route between Carrington and Flixton is often submerged after frequent heavy rainfall. The nearest route across the Mersey is either Crossford Bridge in Stretford or via Irlam and Warburton toll bridge.

The Smithy, Carrington. The blacksmith played a key role in village life and usually took the trade on for the whole of his working life. The street directory for 1860 and 1864 lists the blacksmith for Carrington as a Mr Thomas Wright, and from 1896 to 1940 and beyond as a Mr Harry Blane.

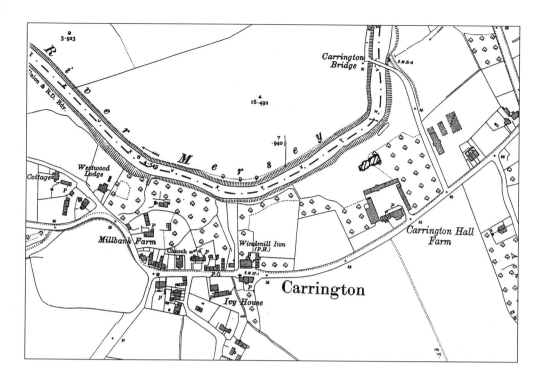

Ordnance Survey map, 1908. This extract shows the centre of the village and the location of Carrington Bridge over the river Mersey.

Windmill Inn, Carrington, 1980s. The Windmill Inn has a long history and was originally used as a courthouse for the Court Baron. The inn was described in a Manchester Journal in 1777: 'at the house of William Burgess, the sign of the Windmill, in Carrington the dwelling house, outbuildings and about 8 acres of land occupied by James Whitehead, Partington from John Owen, Carrington or Mr Worthington, junior.'

The village, Carrington, looking towards Ashton on Mersey. The Methodist chapel can be seen on the right of the photograph.

Cherry Lane, Carrington, 1945. The farm on the left of the photograph is Knathall farm.

A thatched cottage on School Lane, Carrington.

nathall Farm, Carrington, 1945.

St George's church, Carrington. St George's was built between 1757-59 at the expense of Mary, Countess of Stamford. It was dedicated to St George on 1 September 1759. The building is very plain and built of brick in the Flemish style, which was popular at that time. The churchyard, which is surrounded by a low wall, contains the resting place of the first priest of Carrington, the Revd John Foster. Some of the early warden's accounts contain references to everyday life in Carrington: '1795 To Walmsleys for taking down old vane 6 shillings, To Peter Clare to putting up new one 6 shillings, For ale when putting up 3 shillings, 1807 Paid Timothy Brownbill for timber for making new gates for the chapel and putting new weather bird up.'

St George's church, Carrington, showing stone archway and wooden door to the church.

The old schoolhouse, Carrington. The schoolhouse was originally built in 1833 to provide places for 163 children. In 1905 the schoolmaster was a Mr William E. Brereton.

Carrington Road, Carrington, seen here on the left of the picture, was built in 1907 and has since become known locally as the Mile Road, although in fact it does not measure a true mile. The bend in the river Mersey, which can be seen on the middle left of the photograph, is the site of the old iron bridge, which connected Carrington to Flixton. The stumps of the old bridge can still be seen today.

Carrington village in the early 1900s showing a delightful village scene: the woman is holding out her arms to welcome the child, while a gentleman passes the time sitting on the wall and in the distance is a horse and carriage. The building on the right is a shop, which sold general goods. The road is neatly cobbled. The Methodist church, which was built in 1875, can just be seen in the middle of the picture. The church was also used as a venue for concerts. The events, which were announced in the local newspaper, were described as musical entertainments. The *Chronicle* newspaper on 15 February 1889 reported that ' a musical entertainment will be held in the Primitive Methodist Chapel, Carrington on Saturday, the 16th February'.

Ackers Farm, Carrington. Information taken from the 1881 census tells us that Ackers Farm comprised 185 acres and was farmed by a Mr Thomas Newton and his wife Martha. In 1895, as a result of the death of Thomas Newton, the farm was put up for auction. The auction was held on Thursday 28 November 1895. The farm was described as a large holding comprising twelve powerful draught horses and yearlings, sixteen milch cows and heifers, a store bull, promising bull and heifer calves, seven store pigs, sixty head of poultry, 275 tons of clover grass and meadow hay, and three bays of Garton's Abundance and Dyson's Cutts white oats. The furniture included a mahogany hair-seated sofa, two Spanish mahogany bedsteads with damask hangings, a feather bed with a bolster, a cheese press and a cheese churn, a semi billiard table with balls, cues and marker complete, by Orme and sons, in perfect order.

The river Mersey at Carrington, roughly showing the area where Carrington Hall would have been located, facing the river. The stumps of the iron bridge can still be seen today, and although not very clear in this photograph, are positioned at the bend in the river just before it disappears from view.

Sycamore Cottage, Carrington. The date stone above the door reads 1852.

Corporation Cottages, Carrington.

Ivy Cottage, Carrington, looking towards Partington. The junction seen on the far right of th photograph is School Lane.

Bailey Lane, Partington, 2001. The 1891 census lists the occupiers of Bailey Lane as Richar Whitelegg, signalman; Albert Pollard, engine driver; Mary Hazlehurst, widow; James Harrisor farm labourer; and Charles Ogden, a teamsman.

Redbrook Bridge, Partington. The bridge marks the boundary between Partington and Warburton.

Cottages on Warburton Lane, Partington. The plaque reads, 'White Croft Villas Built 1770 Rebuilt 1902'.

Greyhound Hotel, Partington. This photograph was taken as the original Greyhound hotel was being demolished. The pub had been part of the village for over one hundred years. In 1848 the landlord of the pub was listed as a Mr William Clarke.

Bailey Lane, Partington, 1926.

Station Road, Partington, looking towards the railway bridge. The railway constructed in 1873 by the Cheshire Lines Railway provided a vital link between Partington and Broadheath. Many people found employment on the railway, including signalmen, platelayers and the stationmaster. Although the station has long since gone there are still some visible reminders of the original platform.

Erlam Place, Bailey Lane, Partington.

Lock Lane, Partington, was probably named after Lock Field, and referred to a lock on the river Mersey that ran along the border of Partington prior to the building of the Manchester Ship Canal.

The village green, Partington. This photograph was taken from Hall Lane, looking towards Lock Lane.

The village, Partington, in the 1950s. Seen here on the left is the Eccles Provident Industrial Co-operative Society grocer's shop, which was built sometime during the late 1920s. The King William the Fourth public house can be seen in the distance.

Hall Lane, Partington, showing the gas centre and the post office.

Laburnum Cottages, Chapel Lane, Partington.

Manchester Road, Partington. The local brass band leads the procession through the village.

Chapel Lane, Partington, 1970s. The chapel can be seen on the right.

Erlam Place, Partington.

The Squire Inn, Wood Lane, Partington.

Manchester Road, Partington, 1967, showing the vicarage situated opposite the former King William the Fourth public house.

Mr Thomas Clarke, the owner of Clarke's Nursery.

The old school, Partington – a class photograph taken in the early 1900s. Many of the earliest schools in Partington were attached to the church, where along with religious education, children were taught to read and write. The Congregationalist School was built in 1865 and Partington National School in 1876. The National School originally took around sixty infants but was enlarged to take more in 1899. There was also a private school at Elm House, run by a Miss Erskine. Partington County Primary School was opened in 1958 to replace the old National School. Millbank Junior School opened in 1961, Woodlands in 1966, Our Lady of Lourdes in 1964 and Broadoak Secondary Modern in 1965.

The Manse, Chapel Lane, Partington. The tower was used to keep pigeons. In the year 1923 the incumbent was the Revd William Landsell. After the Manse was demolished a new Catholic church was built on the site.

Partington Primary School class photograph, taken around 1947-48.

Congregational church, Partington, 1920s. Non-Conformity was strong in the Partington area, and in 1715 the Reverend William Harding settled in the area as a minister. A petition was set up to raise funds in order to build a chapel in the village. A plot of land consisting of four roods of moss land was purchased from George Jones, a yeoman, for the sum of thirty shillings. The conveyance was to John Gleave, John Barratt, and Edmond Irlam of Partington, the land to be used to build a meeting-house. By 1861 the congregation stood at eighty for the morning service and 150 for the evening. In 1884 the manual of the Congregational church, Bowdon, reported that 'There is nothing new to report from Partington; the Congregations and the Sunday School keep much as usual, but little spiritual impression seems to be made on the neighbourhood though there is improvement in regularity of attendance and propriety of behaviour. Mr Woodbourne is still without helpers in the Sunday School. A successful Band of Hope is conducted, the Meetings being attended by about 60 persons'.

St Mary's church, Partington. The church of St Mary the Virgin became a listed building in 2001. It was originally built in 1884, at a cost of £3,500, from Runcorn stone in a Gothic style. It consisted of a chancel, nave, south porch and south-east tower with a shingled spire containing three bells. The parish registers date from the year 1884.

Hall Lane, Partington, in the 1960s. The shop seen here on the corner has been used as a shop for well over a hundred years and is still in use today. In 1960 it was a fish and chip shop.

Rose Queen, Erlam Farm, Partington.

The village green, Partington, in the 1900s. A group of children pose for this photograph on the village green. The village grocer's shop, which can be seen on the corner, has gone through many changes of use throughout the years and is still in use today.

Hall Lane, Partington, 1973. The former gas shop has been converted into a music shop.

Chapel House, Chapel Lane, Partington, 1921. The Plant family pose for this photograph in the garden.

The stocks, Partington. The stocks were an ancient form of punishment that thankfully has long since died out. In 1405 an act was passed which stated that stocks were to be situated in every town and village in England. A short stay in the stocks was often the punishment for drunkenness, blasphemy or breaking the Sabbath. By the 1830s the stocks were being used less and less, and eventually their use died out altogether. The villages of Partington, Warburton and Ashton on Mersey still have their stocks in place to remind us of a time when wrongdoers were publicly humiliated.

The stocks, Partington, 1911. The stocks are seen here in their original setting on the village green. The fingerpost points to Dunham and Altrincham in one direction and to the ferry in the other. The ferry that crossed the river Mersey, and later the Manchester Ship Canal, was a valuable form of transport between Partington, Irlam and Cadishead, and enabled many people to work further afield.

The community centre on Central Road, Partington, was built to accommodate the increase in social functions in the town. Known as Bucklow House, the centre provided a central venue for many functions, such as dances, dramatic performances and club meetings, that had previously been held in local halls.

Haymaking, Partington. Once a familiar scene in Partington, haymaking was a regular feature of the calendar year. Today it is often hard for us to imagine that Partington was once a sparsely populated rural area consisting mainly of small farms entirely surrounded by farmland. This photograph was taken on land now occupied by the gas works. Many of the farms have now gone but they once provided wheat, barley and potatoes for the villagers and nearby local communities. Farms such as Church Farm, Brook Farm, River Lane Farm, Mersey Farm, Erlam Farm, Landfield Farm, Central Farm, Bridge Farm and Orton Farm are a reminder of days now gone.

The original post office in Partington was on Bailey Lane, on the site where the British Legion flats were later erected.

Carnival, Partington, 1925. The carnival was often the annual highpoint of the year in many towns and villages. The day would consist of a parade through the village followed by competitions and games and would culminate in the crowning of the Rose Queen.

Carnival, Partington, August 1928. The annual carnival was a well-attended event in small towns and villages. This one in 1928 features a car show with all the popular cars of the day on display.

Village scene, Partington, 1910. Note the two gentlemen on the four-wheeled bicycle, which was a common form of transport before the motorcar became popular.

Partington station in the early 1900s. The stationmaster and his family pose for this photograph on the station platform. Partington station had a variety of stationmasters throughout, and from 1896 to 1923 Kelly's Directory of Cheshire lists at least four of them, so this photograph may show one of the following: James William Solly (1896), John William Jones (1902), Charles Boyers (1906), Arthur Miller (1910-1923). From the 1930s onwards the Cheshire Lines Railway administered the running of the station, and the directory no longer lists the stationmasters by name.

A pony and trap on the village green, Partington, *c.* 1910.

Partington, looking towards Warburton. Chapel Lane can be seen on the left of the photograph with Bailey Lane on the right. The stocks can be made out on the right, next to the finger post. The old Methodist chapel can be seen on the far left, with the old school visible in the distance.

Wesleyan chapel and school, Warburton Lane, Partington. Like its neighbour Carrington, Partington had a strong non-conformist following and as early as 1779 they were included in the Manchester Preaching Circuit. In 1843 the Partington Wesleyan Methodist Church was founded, with the church building and school being built in 1861.

Manchester Road, Partington, showing the railway bridge, 1976.

Corner of Warburton Lane and Wood Lane, Partington. The school was used as a venue for youth and Scout groups.

Partington Market in the 1960s.

Scroggins Lane, Partington, in the 1970s. The name Scroggins Lane first appears as a street name on the 1881 census, but may be older. This photograph, taken around 1970, shows the entrance to the caravan park.

Hall Lane, Partington, in the 1970s. Hall Lane takes its name from Partington Hall, which was once situated in this area. The railway bridge can be seen on the left.

Warburton Lane, Partington, looking towards Warburton. Nowadays Warburton Lane is a busy thoroughfare with traffic travelling through to Carrington Spur and the motorway. This photograph was taken in the days when roads were much quieter.

Scroggins Lane, Partington.

Partington County Primary School, 1959. Can you recognize anyone in this photograph?

Moss Lane, Partington, in the 1960s.

Kilnbutts Terrace, situated on Scroggins Lane, Partington. The date stone reads 1889.

The King William the Fourth, Partington. In January 2002 the King William the Fourth public house was finally demolished after being left empty for some time. The pub, which was over 200 years old, had a long history as a coaching house. It was known locally as the King Billy and was a well-known local landmark.

The King William the Fourth, Partington, as it looked in 1977.

Four

The Manchester Ship Canal

During the nineteenth century Manchester's economy had been revolutionized and was in great need of an outlet to the sea other than the river Mersey, to enable it to trade on a competitive basis. Local trade had suffered due to the high price of rail transport and the cost of passing goods through Liverpool. The aftermath of the American Civil War, which had affected the cotton industry generally and that of Lancashire in particular, was still being felt. The building of the Manchester Ship Canal marked an era of prosperity and growth that banished finally the depression of local trade.

The canal was $35\frac{1}{2}$ miles long and 26ft deep. It took eleven and a half years to complete, from its conception to its opening – the latter took place on New Years Day in 1894, the canal having been filled by the morning of 25 November 1893. At the time it was considered the greatest canal in the country and was a truly amazing feat of engineering. The canal used the waters of the rivers Irwell, Mersey and Bollin along with other small streams, and in some places used the riverbed as its base. The canal was originally to be constructed in nine sections but was eventually reduced to eight: Eastham to Ellesmere Port, Elsmere Port to Ince, Ince to Runcorn, Runcorn to Norton, Norton to Latchford. Latchford to Warburton, Warburton to Irlam and Irlam to Manchester. The section that concerns us is the Warburton to Irlam section, which covers Partington and Carrington.

The excavation involved the removal of 51 million cubic yards of earth both by men and machinery. The men often lived in purpose-built villages near to the canal and worked long hours. At its height the company employed 16,341 men and boys, many of whom put their lives at risk – indeed there were first aid stations along the canal route, and three hospitals were also built. Between 1888 and 1893 there were over 3000 serious accidents.

The river Mersey provided an idyllic backdrop for Warburton, Partington and Carrington, but was also an important trading route and would have been a busy, living river even before the Manchester Ship Canal was built. A special boat was built to cope with the 'cuts', which were short stretches of man-made canal that avoided the twists and turns of the river. These were first of all powered by the wind and later pulled by horses. Eventually the boats were steam driven. The banks of the Mersey were raised in the early part of the eighteenth century in an attempt to prevent flooding.

Warburton owes its existence to the river Mersey on whose banks it lies. The surrounding countryside was impassable for much of the year and the main means of access to Warburton was by water along the river Mersey. The river could be crossed by means of Hollins ferry, which lay north of the village and operated between Hollins Green and Warburton. It is said that the Duke of Cumberland pursued Bonnie Prince Charlie over the Mersey at this point as the Prince was retreating to Scotland. There was also a ford near Warburton Mill.

The river also provided opportunity for social occasions. The river Mersey at this point was a good straight stretch of water, and as such was used for the Warrington Regatta. The river flowed at the bottom of the rectory garden and it is said that many parties took place there.

In 1863 a stone toll bridge was built over the river by the Rixton and Warburton Bridge Company, and the ferry was closed. Only thirty years later, the Manchester Ship Canal was built and the old bridge was used as part of the road to the high level bridge which now crosses the canal, still acting as a toll bridge. The dried bed of the Mersey can be seen from this bridge. The canal is at its narrowest on the stretch from Warburton to Mill Bank in Partington. Here it is only 90ft wide whereas most of the rest of the canal is 120ft wide.

The cutting of the Manchester Ship Canal provided a much-needed route to the seaport of Liverpool, and it must have been a strange sight indeed to see large cargo ships passing through the countryside. The building of the Warburton section of the canal was not without its problems. In 1888 a flood occurred which stopped work and buried machinery. A more serious accident was a landslide that occurred in April 1889. The slide sank a steam wagon under tons of mud, the cost of the damage being put at £2,000.

The work on the Manchester Ship Canal affected the railway network of the area and required the diversion of the lines over high bridges, so as to enable larger ships to traverse the canal. According to Paul Bolger, in his *History of the Cheshire Lines Committee*, the Cheshire Lines Railway was an amalgamation of the West Cheshire Railway, the Stockport, Timperley and Altrincham Junction Railway and the Liverpool Central Station Railway. Places other than Manchester benefited from the railway and canal. Stockport had a booming cotton industry with no access to a port, so the railway was invaluable in the transportation of goods to Liverpool. The Skelton West to Partington junction was opened in 1873, with Partington station opening in 1874. When the Manchester Ship Canal was cut, the company railway line between Glazebrook and Partington, which had opened in 1893, was moved over and raised to go over the canal. The original route was given over to the Manchester Ship Canal Railway to accommodate the Partington coaling basin. This necessitated the construction of a new passenger station at Partington.

The Partington section of the Manchester Ship Canal was very important. The canal was widened there to enable ships to dock and refuel, and it became a vital export station. Partington was the nearest port to the coalfields of Lancashire, Derbyshire, Staffordshire and parts of Yorkshire, and as exports rose during the period 1904-07 Partington was extended annually. The coal was loaded straight from the railway on to the ships. Partington became a great railway depot thanks to this trade in coal and other commodities such as cotton. As coal-fired industries declined, the coaling basins at Partington were adapted to handle other products such as chemicals.

The Manchester Ship Canal at Carrington was also linked to the railway system. When Carrington Moss was chosen for the dumping of night soil and other waste as a way of coping with Manchester's population boom in the nineteenth century, transport of the refuse was to be done by both rail and water. A light railway system was built and a wharf area on the then river Mersey was proposed. The Moss belonged to the Earl of Stamford and it was sold to the Manchester Corporation on 5 August 1886. A level crossing was constructed over Partington Lane (Manchester Road) with gates on either side of the road. The Canal Company closed the Mersey and Irwell Navigation on 11 April 1888 and for the next few years the refuse was moved entirely by rail. In March 1899 however, the Manchester Ship Canal Company constructed a temporary dock on the canal and made a wharf over the bank. The trams were lowered down the slope by a steam winch and the refuse was transferred by hand. The Manchester Ship Canal Company offered compensation to the Manchester Corporation, which took some time to negotiate. However, the Company was finally given an area at the new Carrington Wharf. In the years after the building of the Manchester Ship Canal sixty-eight per cent of the refuse moved was done so via the canal.

Warburton church with the river Mersey running beside it as it must have looked after the building of the Manchester Ship Canal. There is a boat on the river and the tall chimneys of the rectory can be seen behind the trees.

A sailing flat on the river Mersey. This type of boat was built particularly to navigate the twists and turns of the river. They were sometimes drawn by horses, and were eventually replaced by the steamboat. Photograph courtesy of E.J. Morton Publishers.

The dry bed of the old river Mersey. The Manchester Ship Canal and the river Mersey share the same path for some of this stretch, but the old riverbed can be seen from the toll bridge.

Opposite top: The cutting of the Manchester Ship Canal at Warburton. Notice the interesting strata on the side of the canal cutting. Bosdin Leech in his *History of the Manchester Ship Canal* comments that these ripple marks were the oldest that had been found to date in the cutting of the canal. Work on this section started in 1888.

Bottom: A general plan of the Manchester Ship Canal. This plan shows the course of the canal, the river Mersey and the railway systems. From *Engineering*, 26 January 1894.

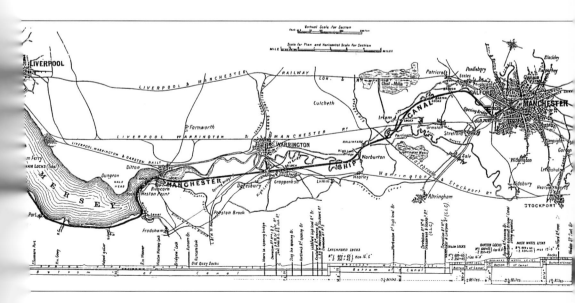

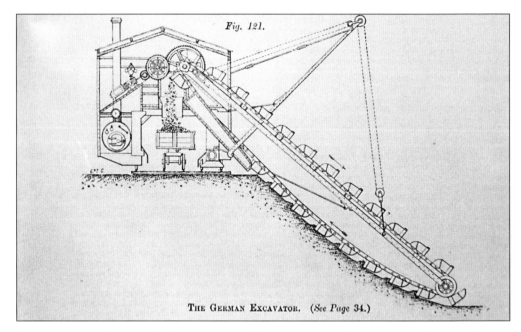

Fig. 121.

THE GERMAN EXCAVATOR. (*See Page 34.*)

Drawing of a German land excavator. This machine, which was made by Lubecker Maschinenbau-Gesellschaft, was generally known as the 'Lubecker' by the engineers, or the 'German' by the workmen. Three of these machines were used on the canal. They required a heavy road and the railway went straight through the hub of the machine. The material was scooped up into buckets that came round and deposited the earth in trucks at the top of the incline (the bank of the canal). Tree trunks and large boulders could not be dealt with by this machine, so they had to be removed previously.

Excavator at Partington, 1891. Mill Bank mill and lock are in the background. This photograph shows the machine deepening the river Mersey from 6ft to 26ft, which was the depth needed for the canal. Photograph courtesy of E.J. Morton Publishers.

Land excavator in use on the workings of the Ship Canal. From *Engineering*, 26 January 1894.

Canoe found in the bed of the river Mersey at Partington. This canoe was found when the Manchester Ship Canal was being constructed in 1890. It is thought to be prehistoric. Photograph courtesy of E.J. Morton Publishers.

Construction of the cantilever bridge over the Manchester Ship Canal at Warburton. The design of the bridge, according to a report in *Engineering*, 26 January 1894, is the same as that of the Forth Bridge. The bridge was built outwards on both sides from the shore to the ends of the cantilevers, and the middle section was lifted from barges. This bridge had a span of 206ft and the steel used weighed 783 tons. It is 75ft above the water of the canal and is still a toll bridge. The roadway is 18ft wide and the pavement 3ft 6ins wide. The bridge saves a long journey round via either Barton or Warrington for those wanting to cross the canal from the nearby towns.

Warburton Bridge. The arches of the old bridge were filled up to strengthen the new bridge in 1910. From *Engineering*, 26 January 1894.

Warburton Old Bridge. This original toll bridge was built by the Rixton and Warburton Bridge Company in 1863 at a cost of £550, which was to be retrieved by means of a toll. The company was also responsible for the repair of the bridge. The Rixton and Warburton Bridge Act of 1863 states that the bridge 'shall not be deemed a county bridge… The bridge shall be maintained and kept in repair by the company'. When the new bridge was built on the back of the old, the toll was still enforced. Photograph courtesy of E.J. Morton Publishers.

Warburton toll bridge. The new bridge was built on the back of this old stone bridge, the arches being filled in to strengthen it. Photograph courtesy of E.J. Morton Publishers.

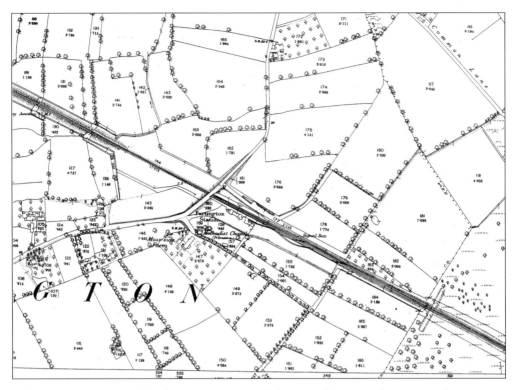

Ordnance Survey map (Cheshire VIII.12, 1874) showing the original position of Partington station.

The old railway line at Partington, marked by the footpath. Partington station opened in May 1874. This original station closed and a replacement station opened in 1893 as the railway was raised to the required height over the Manchester Ship Canal, which was then being cut. The old section of the railway was given over to the Manchester Ship Canal Railway.

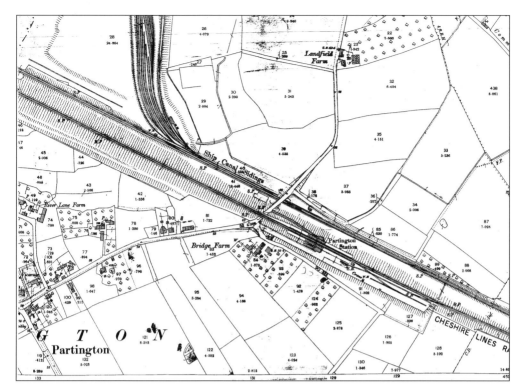

Ordnance Survey map (Cheshire VIII.12, 1898) showing the position of Partington station after it was moved to accommodate the Manchester Ship Canal. This station is further south than the original. As can be seen, the Methodist church is situated much nearer the railway line.

Part of the platform at the new Partington station. This is the end of the platform, as can be seen by the incline. Some of the original brickwork can also be seen.

The old lock chamber and house at Mill Bank in 1970. The original lock was constructed to drive the waterwheel of Ockleston Mill.

Partington ferry in the early 1960s.

Manchester Ship Canal oil leak (courtesy of the *Sale Guardian*, 10 June 1976). The canal was closed in June 1976 when one of the pipelines that carried the oil to Stanlow from Shell at Carrington was fractured. About 2,500 gallons of crude oil leaked into the canal. Ten inward-bound ships and one outward-bound ship were stopped, and a Russian tanker had to be towed away. Fire fighters from Irlam, Sale and the special Shell fire brigade attended the leak and the fire service was on standby until the following day.

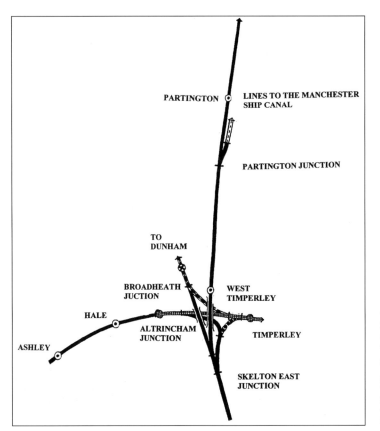

PARTINGTON

LINES TO THE MANCHESTER
SHIP CANAL

PARTINGTON JUNCTION

TO
DUNHAM

BROADHEATH
JUCTION

WEST
TIMPERLEY

HALE

ASHLEY

ALTRINCHAM
JUNCTION

TIMPERLEY

SKELTON EAST
JUNCTION

Railway plan (after Paul Bolger). Plan of the Cheshire Lines Committee railway, showing Partington Junction and the Manchester Ship Canal lines.

IRLAM WHARF

CANAL

Removed by 1906

SHIP

CARRINGTON WHARF

OLD RIVER COURSE

Crane .

Engine Shed & Smithy

Shelter

MANCHESTER

**Carrington Wharf
1896**

Carrington Wharf, 1896, from *Manchester's Narrow Gauge Railways* by Robert Nichols. The wharf was situated on the Manchester Ship Canal at Carrington, behind Corporation Cottages, and was the destination of goods and materials carried by the light railway network across Carrington Moss.

Water tower in Carrington, from *Manchester's Narrow Gauge Railways*. Engines working on the light railway network on the Carrington estate filled up from this water tower, which was on Common Lane, near Asphodel Farm.

Mill Bank Hall. This hall, which was situated on the banks of the Mersey, and later the Manchester Ship Canal, was said to have been the home of the Hargreaves family when the Manchester Ship Canal was being cut at Partington. They objected to the construction of the canal so near to their home saying 'The canal would destroy the amenities and privacy of his house, disturb his rookery and possibly cause subsidence of his buildings', and that 'it would put an end to his ferry'. The 1881 census shows both Mill Bank Hall and Mill Bank House as uninhabited. The electoral registers of both 1884 and 1885 show Edward Spencer Hargreaves as living at Mill Bank Hall.

The engine shed and smithy at Carrington Wharf, 1954, from *Manchester's Narrow Gauge Railways*.

Partington coaling basin. This part of the canal was used both for the refuelling of ships and the loading of coal onto the cargo ships. The canal was made wider at this point to accommodate such activity. The wharf at the Partington coaling basin was the longest wharf on the canal, being 4000ft long. The first steamboat to coal at Partington was the *Mersey* and the first passenger to land at the dock was Mr W.E. Appleton.

Five

Industry

Warburton has traditionally been a farming community. We can see on the Tithe map and the census, and in the directories, that the occupation of the inhabitants is predominantly that of farmer. The style of farming changed at the time of the industrial revolution from arable to dairy, and then later back to cultivation, as in later years market gardening came into being and produce was sold in the Manchester markets.

The other industry in Warburton was the mill, which was a natural complement to the farming industry. It is described in the 1864 Directory of Cheshire as an 'extensive flour mill, in the occupation of Mr Shaw, worked by the water of the Bollin, which flows into the Mersey'. In 1994 a boundary change put Warburton Mill within Warrington Metropolitan Borough, it having previously been in Trafford. However, historically, the mill belongs to Warburton.

The date of the corn mill is hard to establish. It is mooted that it dates back to Anglo-Saxon times, but there is no evidence of this. There is also supposed to be a charter by which half of the mill between Warburton and Lymm was given to the Warburton family by Ada of Lymm. This charter has not been traced and is not listed in the catalogue of Warburton charters. However, a mill is mentioned in several charters between 1170 and 1212, when Brother Roger of Cockersand granted a quarter share of the mill at the Bollin to Thomas de Horribi. This makes Warburton Mill one of the earliest examples of a medieval mill site in northern Cheshire.

There is some debate as to the whereabouts of the medieval mill. When the last mill was demolished it was found that the older mill had not stood on the same site, but had probably been located about 40m to the north-east of the later site.

The mill is mentioned in the Warburton rental of 1572, but it is possible that there were other mills in the area. On the Tithe map there are fields in Warburton Park called Mill field, Dam field and Dam of Spring, which straddle a water course that feeds the Mersey. This could mean that there was a mill in this vicinity. There is also a Mill Hill in the Carr Green area on the Tithe map. It is near to a hemp yard and field and it has been suggested that a mill here could have been used to process hemp.

Arnold Drinkwater wrote in his diaries that the mill was rebuilt in 1716, but nobody is sure when the later four-storey building was erected, although it is generally thought to be the late eighteenth or early nineteenth century. The last family to have worked the mill was the Thornley family who rented the site from 1896. In 1931 the family bought the mill from the Wholesale Co-operative Society, who had bought the Warburton estates in 1918, and extended it further. The mill ceased to function in 1991 and was demolished around ten years later. Private dwellings now stand on the site.

In 1916 the Manchester Corporation bought land in the Carrington area with a view to building an electricity power station. There was already a power station at Barton and this would provide them with an additional alternative. However it was not until 1947 that any building work began to take place. In 1948 the British Electricity Authority took over the responsibility for the building of the station and work finally commenced in 1953.

The location, close to the river Mersey boundary and bordering the Manchester Ship Canal, meant that the area was often prone to flooding and investigations were needed to make sure the land was suitable for building on. A borehole investigation indicated that the land was of a variable nature with uncertain bearing capability. To overcome this, 7,850 piles of reinforced concrete were used as foundations before any work could begin on building the station. Water, which was used in the cooling process, was drawn from the Manchester Ship Canal.

Commissioning work on the 130-acre site began in 1953, but the site was not officially opened until 20 July 1956. The opening ceremony was performed by Alderman Sir William Walker. The power station at one time employed over 350 people and the company provided the staff with a sports and social club and also ran a staff football team. A new staff canteen was opened on Monday 18 October 1954.

The station was powered by coal, which was transported in by both rail and road. In 1955, rail strikes presented the station with serious problems as the continuous supply of coal required to run the station became difficult to maintain. In order to keep the station running, a special road was constructed for the coal to be brought in. The site received special attention during the 1960s when the Russian minister for power Georgi Malenkov visited the site.

Carrington power station was famous for its two tall chimneys, which stood 350ft high and could be seen for many miles around. The chimneys had an internal diameter of 18ft at the top, while at the base the brickwork was over 9ft thick. On full output the power station burned over 130 tonnes of coal every hour, and although it had only a short history, it was for a time the oldest coal-fired power station.

In 1940 Petrocarbon Ltd acquired an 800-acre site in the village of Carrington with the purpose of building the first chemical plant in the United Kingdom. Despite opposition from the residents of both Carrington and Sale, the plans were passed and building began in 1947. The boundary for the proposed chemical plant ran from the Windmill Inn in Carrington to the gas works in Partington, and covered most of the village of Carrington.

The building of the chemical plant was to change the face of Carrington village completely and also resulted in the loss of a large amount of arable land and associated farm buildings. Three farmers whose families had farmed the Carrington area for many years lost their farms. Mr Meyer of Carrington Hall Farm lost 258 acres, William Northcott of Ashphodel Farm and Booth Hey Farm lost a large amount of land and Annie Collins of Common Lane Farm lost around 100 acres.

The first plant on the site was constructed between 1947 and 1951 and covered only eighty acres of the 800-acre site. The architects in charge of the work, Scherrer and Hicks, faced special safety problems. Wood was a fire hazard and therefore had to be used as little as possible, while the buildings had to be well spaced. Concrete blocks, which were used in the construction, were made on the site from excavated sand. This left a large pit, over two acres wide and 10ft deep, which was later left to form an artificial lake.

The plant was designed to operate the Catarole process, a high-temperature catalytic cracking process to produce chemicals from Naphtha, a product of crude oil. The crude oil was transported by ship along the Manchester Ship Canal to Partington coaling basin, from where it was pumped via pipeline to the site. Cooling water for the process was taken from the river Mersey.

In 1955 the site was sold to Shell Chemicals, part of the Royal Dutch Shell Group of companies, and was extensively developed and modified. Pipelines from the Shell oil refinery at Stanlow, near Ellesmere Port, were laid to connect the two sites. The pipelines were over twenty-three miles long and are still in use today. During the 1960s the site expanded rapidly and became a 'mini town'. It had its own power stations (two of), fire station, medical centre (with ambulance), offices, laboratories, restaurants, workshops and training centre. Over 3000 people were employed on the site, which became the hub of the local economy. The two chimneys on the east and central power stations, along with the massive flare stack, became well-known landmarks. Both the chimneys were demolished in the 1980s but the flare stack is still there, being an essential part of the site safety system.

The recession of the 1980s hit the chemical industry hard and in order to remain competitive Shell embarked on a restructuring program for the site, which in turn meant a reduction in the size of the workforce. From the heady days of the 1960s, when over 3000 people worked on the site, by the late 1980s the workforce numbered just 498. Furthermore, Shell sold off one of the plants and a new name, the Huntsman Chemical Company, became part of the site alongside that of Shell Chemicals. Change was the order of the day, and the training centre and lecture theatre, along with several office blocks and outbuildings were cordoned off from the rest of the site to become Carrington Business Park, an area for new and existing small to medium-sized businesses to set up and develop.

In the 1990s, due to company mergers, Shell Chemicals at Carrington became Montell, while at the same time one of the plants was taken over by the Elenac group and the Huntsman Chemical Company became Nova Chemicals. In 2000, Montell and Elenac were subject to another change and a new name – Basell UK – now governs the site. At the time of writing, February 2002, Basell employs around 200 people on the site and Nova Chemicals around 100, a far cry from the 3000-plus of the 1960s.

The Air Products plant was built during the 1960s to produce oxygen, nitrogen, argon and carbon dioxide. In 1976 Trafford MBC approved the plans for a 21m-high cylindrical tank to be built, on the condition that the company carried out landscaping work to shield the tank from St George's church, Carrington, which was a listed building.

The history of Partington paper mill can be traced back to 1732, when Mr John Barratt, a landowner in Partington, sold $38\frac{3}{4}$ perches of land to the Old Quay Navigation Company for the purpose of building a weir and a lock across the river Mersey. The lock was known as Ullarts Nest lock. In 1755 the Old Quay Navigation Company sold a portion of the land to Mr Ellis Crompton, whose intention was to build a paper mill, for the small sum of £2 18s. The original paper mill was a single-storey building powered by water drawn from the river Mersey through two underground tunnels. The mill was partitioned so that it could also be used as a residence for the mill manager and his family. The mill produced a type of paper known as 'rope brown', which was extremely strong and was to become a speciality of the mill until 1906.

By 1800 the mill had changed hands three times. In 1762 Abraham Titley, who owned a nearby silting and rolling mill, bought the mill for £855. Mr Titley was responsible for the construction of the 'Old Building', a finishing room with a loft above, and a separate dwelling house and summerhouse for himself and his family. After his death the mill, including the slitting and rolling mill, was sold to Mr Thomas Lyon for £3,500. Mr Lyon made further improvements to the dwelling house and also provided a separate house for his foreman, who at that time was a Mr Thomas Greaves. Thomas Greaves was made a partner in the mill up until the death of Mr Lyon in June 1781.

The river Mersey at that time was plentiful with fish of all kinds and on one occasion it was reported that Thomas Greaves caught over 208lbs of salmon. It was common for the fish to swim into the tunnels, where they then became trapped. The ownership of the mill then passed to Mr Lyon's sister Elizabeth and her husband Mr Kerfoot.

In 1793 the mill was transferred from waterpower to steam power, an engine house was built and a steam engine installed. In 1796 the slitting and rolling mill business was transferred from Partington to Liverpool, and the old premises were utilized as corn mills. When Mr Kerfoot died in 1808, James Greaves, the son of the foreman Thomas Greaves, bought the mill.

James Greaves then took his nephew Thomas Occleston into partnership, and when he died, Thomas took full control of the company. Thomas Occleston was the son of a courier and tanner from Mere and was also responsible for the building of a new tannery and bone manure works at Massey Brook in Cheshire. He bought the site of the old corn mill, built a paper mill there, enlarged the two old tunnels, installed new water wheels and new machinery and spent a large amount of money on modernization.

The Occleston family were to own the mill for over ninety-eight years, and during this period they divided their time between Mill Bank Hall and another residence at Massey Brook. In 1864 Morris's street directory indicates that Thomas Occleston and his family were living at Mill Bank Hall while his son Robert Occleston was living at Mill Bank House.

On many occasions the mill was burned down, but it was always rebuilt. In 1906 the mill employed around 100 people and produced an output of around sixty-five tons of paper per week. The paper it produced included the old rope brown, yellow grocery brown, envelopes, reel and bag papers and the new 'Kraft' paper, which had been previously imported from Scandinavia. On Saturday 23 December 1906, the owners and workers of the mill celebrated the 150th anniversary of the mill with festivities. These celebrations were held at the Saracen's Head in Warburton. Among those present were Mr T. Occleston, Dr Jago, M. George Worthington, Mr Anderson and another Mr Worthington, as well as many workers from the mill. Everyone sat down to a hearty meal, which was then followed by dancing and a firework display.

Up to the First World War the Occleston family mainly employed people who lived in the Partington area, but the shortage of labour which followed the war changed all that and more people who lived much further afield began to be employed. Both men and women worked in the mill, often working for long hours, which were based around a continuous shift system. There was no time off for lunch, which was eaten while on the job. The men were employed in the operation of the machinery while the women worked on the finished paper, cutting it into sizes and sorting it into stacks. The mill continued manufacturing paper until the late 1960s when it finally closed after two disastrous fires. The mill was still in use up to 1964 (Ordnance Survey map SJ7091), but by 1972 was listed as disused. It was eventually demolished sometime during the early 1970s.

The tannery was situated on Wood Lane in Partington. The hides, which were brought in from the abattoir in Manchester, were transported either by water, along the Bridgewater Canal to Burford Wharf, or by road. The tannery is mentioned on the census of 1861 as Tanyard Farm, and can be seen on the Ordnance Survey map of 1896 for Lancashire (sheet number CX.9). During the 1920s a leather factory was also established in the old smithy premises. Tool bags and industrial gloves were produced using the leather supplied by the tannery. By the 1940s the tannery was no longer used and was replaced by a paint works.

Partington gas works was built during the late 1920s by Manchester Corporation as a direct result of the increased demand for fuel by the city of Manchester. It was officially opened on 8 May 1929 and covered over 175 acres in total. The site was selected because of its proximity to the Manchester Ship Canal, which allowed for the easy transport of coal, used in the production of gas. Partington was a quiet, rural village with only a few houses and farms, so a 'mini village' had to be constructed in order to provide houses for the future workforce that would be employed in the gas works. A total of thirty-one new houses were built, including a detached house for the foreman.

Partington coaling basin on the Manchester Ship Canal was created so that coal taken from the Lancashire and Yorkshire coalfields would have an access point to the sea, and at the same time provide a refuelling stop for ships. The Manchester Ship Canal at this point was wider than elsewhere, measuring 250ft across. This extra width allowed ships to dock on either side without interfering with other vessels passing along the canal. The coal was brought from the coalfields to the coaling basin by a rail link that was specially constructed for the purpose; the northern link was through Partington and the southern link through Glazebrook. On arrival at the coaling basin the coal was off-loaded via hoists, which lifted the coal-carrying trucks, each weighing around 19 tons, to a height of over 26ft before tipping the contents. Each hoist had two sidings, one for the trucks carrying coal, the other for the empty trucks. The movement of the empty trucks was enabled by gravity – as they were now positioned at a greater height, they would descend to the end of the siding.

Both Carrington and Partington, though heavily industrialized, still relied on farming. The land was very fertile with a peat base, ideal for growing wheat, barley, oats, hay and potatoes. Many of the farms have now gone, but some of the road names remind us of times gone by. Many of the farms employed Irish labourers who would arrive in the early spring and stay until October. A reminder of some of the early farms are Erlam Farm, Bridge Farm, Landfield Farm, Orton Farm, Wark Farm, Rivers Lane Farm, Partington Hall Farm, Mersey Farm, Central Farm, Broadoak Farm and Brook Farm.

Warburton Corn Mill. This, the southern wall of the main four-storey mill block, was the earliest and largest part of the complex. This photograph shows the site of the headrace, which was the part of the river that turned the mill wheels, and we can also see the sluice gate on the left and weir on the right.

The mill site as it is today. The mill was demolished in 2000 and modern apartments were built.

The mill pool, or tail race, as it is today.

The stone bridge over the river Bollin at Warburton. This bridge was originally built in 1664 to replace a wooden bridge, which in turn replaced a ford at this point on the river. According to Arnold Drinkwater, who was the bailiff to the Warburton family at this time, the laying of the flags cost 60s, and in 1700 another 25s was spent on improving the bridge.

The weir across the Bollin during the building of the apartments that now stand there.

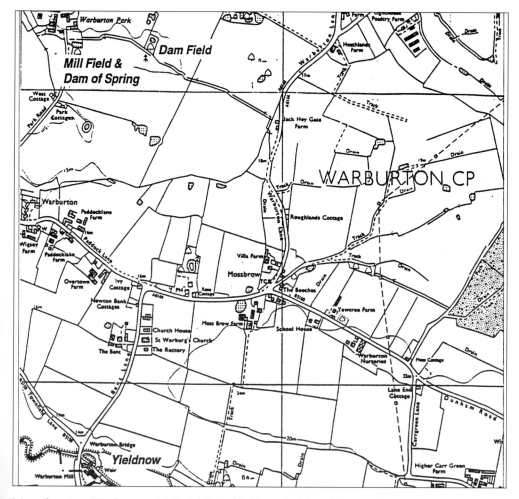

Map showing Warburton Mill, Mill Field, Dam Field and Dam of Spring, courtesy of Dr M. Nevell.

Aerial photograph of Shell Chemicals, Carrington, 1 February 1968. The photograph shows Shell Chemicals in its heyday. To the left of the road can be seen the chemical plants, while to the right are all the administration buildings. The road that can be seen running along the bottom of the photograph is Isherwood Road. Carrington village can be seen on the right of the photograph with some housing under construction at the bottom of the picture. The Manchester Ship Canal and Partington gas works can be seen at the top of the photograph.

Shell Chemicals, Carrington, 1982. The main gates of the Shell Chemicals site were situated on Manchester Road, Carrington.

Shell Chemicals, Carrington. The new railway line at Shell Chemicals, photographed in January 1977.

Carrington power station in 1954. The power station was flooded in 1954 when an exceptionally high incoming tide further along the river Mersey caused the Manchester Ship Canal to burst its banks.

Aerial photograph of Partington, taken on 1 February 1968, showing the houses and main shopping area of Partington. The King William the Fourth pub is the white building at the bottom left of the picture. The gas works and Shell Chemicals are in the centre with Urmston just discernable in the top left corner.

The old railway track, Carrington. The railway track, once part of an old tramway, ran through Carrington Moss to Carrington. It has been disused for many years and today looks more like a country lane.

124

Carrington power station. The two chimneys, which stood around 350ft in height, could be seen for many miles and were a local landmark.

Partington gas works, showing a damaged gas tank.

Manchester Road, Partington. Partington gas works can be seen on the far right of the photograph.

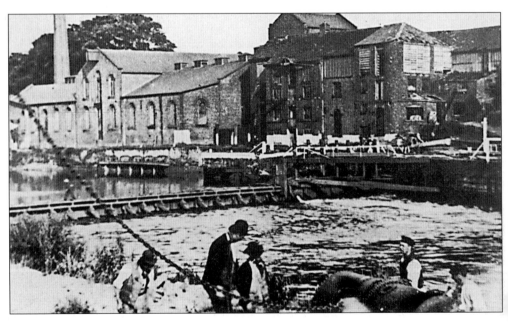

Millbank Paper Mill, Partington, 1890. Work on the Manchester Ship Canal had started in earnest. This photograph shows the weir across the river Mersey before the river was diverted into the Ship Canal. Photograph courtesy of E.J. Morton Publishers.

Wood Lane, Partington, 1967. The paint works was established in Partington during the 1920s and is listed in Kelly's 1928 Directory of Cheshire as 'Williams, John E and Co. Ltd. paint, colour and varnish manufacturers (wholesale and export)'.

Train at Partington coaling basin, 1955. The driver of the locomotive seen here in the photograph is Mr Bert Etchells, and the guard is Mr Brian Potts.

The paper mill, Partington. The paper is neatly stacked, ready for distribution. Both men and women were employed in the factory, often working long hours without a break.

Manchester Ship Canal, Partington. This photograph was taken from the site of the old paper mill, the remains of which can be seen in the foreground. In the distance we can see the metal railway bridge between Flixton and Irlam.